Logee's Greenhouses

Spectacular

Container Plants

Logee's Greenhouses

Brugmansia

Spectacular
Container Plants

How to Grow Dramatic Flowers for Your Patio, Sunroom, Windowsill, and Outdoor Spaces

By Byron E. Martin and Laurelynn G. Martin

Willow Creek® PRESS

MINOCQUA, WISCONSIN

Dedicated to Joy Logee Martin and Richard Logee.
and in memory of Dad, Ernest Evans Martin
— B.E.M.

For Murm and Gramp
Their love, always in flower.
— L.G.M.

Published by Willow Creek Press, P.O. Box 147, Minocqua, Wisconsin 54548
For information on other Willow Creek Press titles, call 1-800-850-9453

Designed by Pat Linder
Edited by Andrea Donner

Library of Congress Cataloging-in-Publication Data
Martin, Byron E.
    Logee's Greenhouses spectacular container plants : how to grow dramatic
    flowers for your patio, sunroom, windowsill, and outdoor spaces / Byron E.
    Martin and Laurelynn G. Martin.
        p. cm.
    ISBN 1-57223-399-0 (hardcover)
    1. Container gardening. 2. Plants, ornamental.   I. Martin, Laurelynn G.
II. Title.
    SB418 .M28 2001
    635.9'86--dc21   2001000690

Printed in Canada
9 8 7 6 5 4 3 2 1

Contents

Acknowledgements

I would like to thank my wife, Laurelynn G. Martin, for undertaking the project through thick and thin; my mother, Joy Logee Martin, and my uncle, Richard Logee, for their many years of dedication to Logee's; without them we would not be who we are today. My thanks go to my brother, Geoffrey Martin, for his support; my cousin, Betty Martin, for traveling the journey with me; Brian Herlin, business manager, for his expertise; Claudia Vincenti Smith, office manager, for her unending support; Debbie Lavoie, head grower, for her green efforts; Virge Lorents for her beautiful photographs; and Don Taylor for his excellent artwork. And, I thank the entire Logee's staff for their outstanding contributions — Growers: Jessica Chevalier, Brenda Jacobs, Robin Montigny, Laurie Robillard, Anna Terwilleger; Shipping department: Rene Bentley, Laurie DeLaRosa, Joanne Harvey, Bethany Kellam; Office staff: Nancy McKeon, Gaina Penrod, Sandy Smith; Lab technicians: Paula Thatcher, Noelle Charron; Retail: Debra Manoogian; and Facilities coordinator: Alan Harvey.

Also, I would like to thank Tasha Tudor for her many years of support and love for our greenhouses.

—Byron E. Martin

I would like to thank first my family for pitching in, and my husband, Byron E. Martin, for his patience and expertise in co-authoring this book. I'd like to thank my children, Elijah and Angelise, for having a few too many macaroni and cheese dinners; my mother-in-law, Joy Logee Martin, for her consulting; and Aunt Fay Smith for her editorial input. My mother and father, Bob and Barbara Glass, for being wonderful grandparents to my kids. My sister, Gwendolyn Carbone, for her editorial skills. My good friend and fellow writer, Patrick McKenna Lynch Smith, for his encouragement and writer's input. Special thanks go to Logee's Greenhouses staff, especially Claudia Vincenti Smith, for her friendship and managerial skills; Brian Herlin, for his computer finesse; Cornelia Waldman, former marketing manager, for her original encouragement. I thank Nancy and Philip Kruger for their friendship and support through many personal crises; Cheryl Placido for her emotional support and the healthy meals; Susan LaRose, massage therapist, who worked on my tired shoulders; Kathleen King for her true words of wisdom; and child care providers and friends, Jo-Anne Gardner, Misty DeLaRosa, and her mom, Laurie DeLaRosa.

Also, I would like to thank Andrea Donner, from Willow Creek Press, for her faith and vision in this project.

—Laurelynn G. Martin

By Joy Logee Martin

Second generation owner, presently 90 years old

Recently, my 92-year-old sister asked me, "Joy, is there any day you do not go to the greenhouses?" My answer was, "I have not *lived* if I do not go to the greenhouses every day!"

Logee's has been my life's work. Our first catalog, published in 1939, was a small list of scented-geraniums. I have loved geraniums since I was a child and my interest in collecting scented-geraniums from around the world paid off. Today, we grow 53 varieties of these fragrant beauties. I also have been interested in herbs, and I am the oldest living member of the National Herb Society of America.

My father started the business in 1872 with a love for fragrant flowers and plants. We had thirteen children in our family; most of us were involved in horticulture. I was the one that stayed behind and took over the family business. When I was young, a dear friend gave me a copy of *Bailey's Encyclopedia* , a three volume set. I started a long study of exotic plants, learning their botanical names and the history of their habitat. I believe I will never finish this study.

At Logee's, we are known for our expansive collection of over 1,500 varieties. My son, Byron, now manages a total of 13 greenhouses and continues to search the globe for new plant introductions. Also, we are known for our begonia collection. We have over 375 varieties of begonias. My brother, Ernest, spent his life hybridizing the dark-leafed, double, sun-loving varieties. One Christmas, I gave him a copy of *Mother Goose* and, lo and behold, the next three begonias that he successfully hybridized he named "Bo Peep," "Lucy Locket," and "Curly Locks."

My heart belongs to Logee's. There was never a time that I did not know the greenhouses. And now I am so pleased that my son, Byron, and my daughter-in-law, Laurelynn, have teamed up to bring you this important book about our tropical and sub-tropical flowering plants. I hope you enjoy the outstanding pictures and our family secrets on how to culture some of our favorites.

— Joy Logee Martin

Camellia

Introduction

To grow tropical flowers is like tending a garden for your soul. Not only are the rewards seen visually, they are also felt by all those who gaze upon the floral form. Many times we hear, "Oh, they are so beautiful but I'm afraid I'd kill it." Fear no more! We have written this book so anyone can grow tropical plants. With a little bit of attention and a willingness to try, container gardening is a joy.

After much demand, we are happy to bring to you *Logee's Greenhouses Spectacular Container Plants*. Daily, our horticultural hotline receives dozens of phone calls with similar questions on plant care addressed throughout this book. Our staff is particularly pleased that we have finally written a reference for the many questions that go along with growing exotic flowers. From the 1,500 varieties that we grow, we have chosen over 200 of the most colorful, fragrant, and unusual specimens.

The book is organized in an easy-to-follow format. The reader can quickly glean the necessary cultural information for each variety and gain valuable knowledge from "Unique Characteristics" and "Other Growing Tips." Not only do we provide information about each family, we also answer general plant care questions under the "Trouble-shooting" section. And we have included detailed chapters about pests, disease, containers, pruning, watering, soils and fertilizers.

The compilation of information has been gathered over three generations. With 109 years of culturing, collecting, and no-nonsense knowledge, we are confident this book will become an invaluable tool for the beginner as well as the experienced container gardener. We have spent years perfecting certain growing techniques, photographing flowers during their optimum blooming cycles, and gathering information from the plants themselves. We are excited to share all of this knowledge with you through this book.

Throughout this process of growing plants, our awareness has shifted. Like many gardeners, we have felt a deep resonance of love and connection when caring for plants, which is not easily explained. We have tried to address the inspirational qualities of the plants as well as their cultural care, and hope the photographs and descriptions of these exquisite plants will make reading this book an enjoyable experience for you.

We hope that you find the container gardening information helpful. But mostly, we hope you find a moment of peace and inspiration as you browse through these pages. Thank you for joining us on a visual, sensual, and instructional journey through *Logee's Greenhouses Spectacular Container Plants*.

—B.E.M. & L.G.M.

Gardenia

Part One

The Plants

Abutilon
Aeschynanthus
Allamanda
Anisodontea
Araujia
Aristolochia
Begonia 'Fibrous'
Begonia 'Rex'
Begonia 'Rhizomatous'
Bougainvillea
Bouvardia
Brugmansia
Brunfelsia
Burbidgea
Calliandra
Camellia
Cantua
Ceropegia
Cestrum
Clerodendrum
Clivia
Costus
Crossandra
Dalechampia
Dichorisandra
Epiphyllum

Eucharis
Euphorbia
Felicia
Fuchsia
Gardenia
Gelsemium
Hardenbergia
Hibiscus
Hoya
Ixora
Jasminum
Justicia
Kalanchoe
Leonotis
Mandevilla
Manetti
Michelia
Mitriostigma
Mucuna
Murraya
Neomarica
Pachystachys
Passiflora
Pavonia
Pelargonium
Pereskia

Phalaenopsis
Phaseolus
Plectranthus
Plumbago
Porphyrocoma
Prostanthera
Pseuderanthemum
Punica
Rondeletia
Ruellia
Russellia
Salvia
Scutellaria
Senecio
Solandra
Stapelia
Stephanotis
Streptocarpus
Stictocardia
Strophanthus
Tabernaemontana
Thunbergia
Trachelospermum
Uncarina
Vigna

Abutilon

Listen carefully, for these bell-shaped blooms send a message of abundant beauty year-round.

BOTANICAL NAME: *Abutilon x Hybridum (a-bew´-ti-lon)*
COMMON NAME: *Flowering Maple or Parlor Maple*
FAMILY NAME: *Malvaceae*
ORIGIN: *Central and South America*

LIGHT: *full to partial sun*
SIZE AND GROWTH: *1 - 3 feet in container; some trailing in habit, most upright growers*
MINIMUM TEMPERATURE: *35°F*
BLOOMING SEASON: *everbloomer with high light levels and when excessive periods of heat are avoided*
OUTSIDE HARDINESS ZONE: *zone 8 and higher; some frost tolerated*
SOIL: *any well-drained potting mix*
BEST TIME TO PRUNE: *anytime growth is excessive for the container*
PESTS OR DISEASE TO WATCH FOR:
 • *insects: high susceptibility to white fly; some susceptibility to aphids and spider mite*
 • *foliar disease: none*
 • *root disease: none*

FERTILIZER: *moderate to heavy amounts of fertilizer year-round*
UNIQUE CHARACTERISTICS/OTHER GROWING TIPS:

Ease of culture makes *Abutilons* one of the most popular choices for first-time gardeners. However, their only limitation is high heat which forces them out of bloom. They will vegetate until cooler weather returns. The upright growers make excellent standards. They are heavy feeders and need a steady supply of fertilizer, especially when kept in a pot. If they are under-fertilized, their leaves will become light colored. The whole plant will look scraggly and may even experience leaf drop. Another tip for *Abutilon* care is to perform preventative spraying for white fly when brought indoors after the outdoor growing season. Or we recommend a hard pruning, taking off all the foliage, which will eliminate pest problems.

Abutilons have a long and colorful history, much like their blooms. They are known as "Parlor Maples" or "Flowering Maples" and have been popular since Victorian times. Their adaptability to cool houses in the Victorian era made these a favorite, especially because of their non-stop show of flowers. Today, they're as popular as ever and in this genus alone, one can grow weeping baskets or exquisite standards. Choose from a variety of color and floral structures — small bells to open-face blooms — and variegated leaves. *Abutilons* are a perfect choice for a beginning gardener.

In the late 1800s, when Logee's was in the cut-flower business, Grandfather Logee used Flowering Maples in all his arrangements, whether corsage, wedding or funeral work. He found that the prolific blooms were always talked about long after the event was over.

The weeping, cascading growth habit of *A*. 'Kentish Bell', *A*. 'Linda Vista Peach', or *A*. 'Huntington Pink' make excellent standards and hanging baskets. Varieties such as *A*. 'Mobile Pink', or *A*. 'Kristen's

Above: Abutilon 'Mobile Pink'; top right: Abutilon 'Bartley Schwartz'; lower right: Abutilon 'Kristen's Pink'

Pink', *A.* 'Clementine', *A. pictum* 'Thompsonii' or *A.* 'Moonchime' have a compact growth habit, an upright stature, and fill the windowsill with abundant blooms and color year-round. With a little attention to fertilization, watering, and light level, these "Flowering Maples" bring cheer and warmth to any "parlor." They add color and fullness to any window box or outdoor planting when used as an annual.

When *Abutilons* are planted directly into the ground in greenhouses or warmer climates, they can grow for many years and will bloom continuously, reaching heights of eight to ten feet. Ease of culture and abundance of bloom make *Abutilons* one of the most popular choices for first-time gardeners.

abutilon

Aeschynanthus

Cascading red blooms give passion and vitality, expressing the endless possibilities of creation.

BOTANICAL NAME: *Aeschynanthus (ie-skee-nan´-thus)*
COMMON NAME: *Lipstick Plant*
FAMILY NAME: *Gesneriaceae*
ORIGIN: *Old Word, Malaysia, India, New Guinea*

LIGHT: *partial light to shade; bright, direct light of the morning or afternoon sun is best, but needs to be shaded from the noonday sun*
SIZE AND GROWTH: *4 - 5 inches in container; trailing in habit*
MINIMUM TEMPERATURE: *60°F*
BLOOMING SEASON: *intermittent bloomer throughout the year; A. obconicus is a winter bloomer*
OUTSIDE HARDINESS ZONE: *zone 10 and higher*
SOIL: *light soil mix, needs to be open and porous; commercial soilless mixes work well*
FERTILIZER: *moderate amounts of fertilizer applied monthly or bimonthly*
BEST TIME TO PRUNE: *after the flowering cycle is complete*

PESTS OR DISEASE TO WATCH FOR:
- *insects: resistant to most insects; occasional mealy bug problems*
- *foliar disease: none*
- *root disease: if kept too wet*

UNIQUE CHARACTERISTICS/OTHER GROWING TIPS:
Tolerant to low light levels, low humidity and erratic watering, *Aeschynanthus* thrives in the harsh conditions of a home. Do not expose to extended periods of cooler temperatures, below 60°F, or the plant will be damaged. *Aeschynanthus* does well as a hanging basket. When its trailing branches grow to great lengths over the edge, the branches or stems can be pruned. This will thicken the growth and maintain the size. *A. obconicus* is a winter bloomer and brings cheer to the darkest days of the year. However, it can be a bit more challenging to grow because it is more sensitive to environmental conditions, such as temperature and fertilization.

Aeschynanthus are well noted for their showy flowers and ability to take the harsh conditions of a home. Their epiphytic nature and native habitat of a dry season are perfect for the forgetful gardener. Dry soil between waterings does not harm or prevent spectacular displays.

A few years back, we found *Aeschynanthus radicans* hanging in

Right: Aeschynanthus radicans; left: Aeschynanthus 'Tiger Stripe'

the corner of a local business office. Obviously, this plant had been forgotten for a couple of weeks. In dire need of a drink, the office staff was accommodating.

The next day, we received a phone call informing us that the plant had made a fast and full recovery and would not be going out to the dumpster after all.

aeschynanthus

Allamanda

The rich colors and floral form are a reminder of the gentle strength that radiates through love.

BOTANICAL NAME: *Allamanda* (al-a-man´-da)
COMMON NAME: *Allamanda*
FAMILY NAME: *Apocynaceae*
ORIGIN: *South America*

Allamanda violacea 'Chocolate Cherry'

LIGHT: *full sun*
SIZE AND GROWTH: *grows 3 - 5 feet in a container; vining in habit*
BLOOMING SEASON: *A. cathartica 'Flore Plena' and A. violacea 'Chocolate Cherry' bloom March through November in the north,* and are everbloomers in the south; *A. cathartica 'Williamsii' is an everbloomer*
MINIMUM TEMPERATURE: *60°F*
OUTSIDE HARDINESS ZONE: *zone 10 and higher*
SOIL: *any well-drained potting mix*
Fertilizer: *moderate levels of fertilizer during active growth; restrict fertilizer during the winter months if light levels are low and temperatures cool. May need to add iron chelate to fertilizer if signs of iron chlorosis appear.*
BEST TIME TO PRUNE: *late winter or early spring, or anytime growth is excessive. Do not prune off all the foliage, especially when not in active growth. Allamandas recover quickly when some foliage is left.*
PESTS OR DISEASE TO WATCH FOR:
• *insects: some susceptibility to white fly and spider mite late in growing season*
• *foliar disease: none*
• *root disease: highly susceptible*

UNIQUE CHARACTERISTICS/ OTHER GROWING TIPS:
Do not become alarmed if some of the leaves yellow in the wintertime and drop. As long as the roots are healthy, you can be assured this is a normal resting period. To avoid root rot, we graft *A.* 'Flore Plena' to a bush-type Allamanda, called *A. neurifolia*, which is not as susceptible to root rot. This controls root disease and makes a strong specimen. *Allamandas* suffer if exposed to extended periods of cold. Keep at 60°F for healthy specimens.
WINTERING OVER: When *Allamandas* are first brought inside, we recommend pruning any excessive growth so they will fit comfortably into their winter growing space. Give them a warm, sunny exposure so some growth will continue during the shortest days of the year.

Allamandas are spectacular plants for those who love fragrance, showy flowers, and versatility. For instance, *Allamanda*

above: Allamanda cathartica 'Williamsii'; *right: Allamanda cathartica* 'Flore Plena'

cathartica 'Flore Plena' not only has an enticing fragrance, but also boasts a brilliant yellow, double-bloom with a ruffle. Its stiff-stemmed vine does excellent on a trellis or stake and, in the southern zones, can be planted directly into the ground.

Another *Allamanda, cathartica* 'Williamsii', also known as the "Golden Trumpet," is especially admired at Logee's as it weaves back and forth across our trellised ceiling, creating a blanket-like effect. These cheery yellow flowers, which have a light fragrance at night, are always in abundant supply. And for those who appreciate a sculptured form, *A.* Williamsii makes a wonderful standard.

In the northern climates, *Allamandas* are adaptable to outdoor growth in the summertime. In the southern climates, they suc-cessfully grow year-round outside. When cultured in a pot or planted directly in the ground, *Allamandas* need some type of support. Give them the freedom to vine and climb and they will add a whole new dimension to your outdoor or indoor living space.

Anisodontea

Soft pink flowers spring forth in a burst of sunshine inspiring a connection to all that matters.

BOTANICAL NAME: *Anisodontea x hypomandarum*
(a-nee-so-dont´-ee-a)
COMMON NAME: *African Mallow*
FAMILY NAME: *Malvaceae*
ORIGIN: *unkown*

LIGHT: *full sun*
SIZE AND GROWTH: *2 - 4 feet in container; upright growth habit*
MINIMUM TEMPERATURE: *40°F*
BLOOMING SEASON: *year-round, except where light levels drop, then reliably in the spring, summer and fall*
OUTSIDE HARDINESS ZONE: *zone 9 and higher*
SOIL: *any well-drained potting mix; will tolerate most soils*
FERTILIZER: *moderate amounts of fertilizer at regular intervals except when light levels are low, then reduce feed or they can get leggy in appearance*
BEST TIME TO PRUNE: *mid-to-late winter pruning will encourage flowering for spring; prune anytime growth is excessive. If plant gets too large by summertime, prune again. Responds well to severe pruning.*

PESTS OR DISEASE TO WATCH FOR:
• *insects: high susceptibility to white fly; some susceptibility to spider mite*
• *foliar disease: none*
• *root disease: some root and stem rot during the heat of the summer, usually because of excessive fertilizer or improper watering*

UNIQUE CHARACTERISTICS/OTHER GROWING TIPS:
Although rapid growers and heavy feeders, do not over water. If the roots are left soggy in the heat of the summer, then the stem and root disease cut off the water supply to the rest of the plant. The African Mallow can then simply collapse and experience "Sudden Death Syndrome." We recommend the use of clay pots because they dry out better. After a hard pruning, do not water as much because their requirements are less. To create a thick, bush-like specimen, wait until the young plant has grown four to five inches, then pinch the tops. Repeat this one more time and you will be well on your way to a beautiful, full plant. When attention is given to watering and fertilization, African Mallow is a plant that rewards with an abundance of rich, brilliant colors from spring to fall.

The African Mallow is a profuse bloomer and literally smothers itself with bright pink flowers. In the height of flowering, one can hardly see the foliage. At Logee's, we often recommend this variety for those wanting to try standard culture. It's a straight grower and

Anisodontea x hypomandarum

branches easily. In as little as one year's time, African Mallow displays a full bushy crown.

Besides making a great standard, African Mallow makes an excellent windowsill plant and is a wonderful choice for the patio. For those with limited space, prune regularly to make a nice compact container plant. Blooming three of the four seasons, this cheerful plant is a welcome addition to any home.

Araujia

The pure sweet flowers and delightful fragrance encourages one to find the sweetness in life.

Araujia Sericofera

BOTANICAL NAME: *Araujia sericofera (a-row´-hee-a)*
COMMON NAME: *Cruel Plant*
FAMILY NAME: *Asclepiadaceae*
ORIGIN: *South America*

LIGHT: *full to partial sun*
SIZE AND GROWTH: *1 - 3 feet in container; vining in habit*
MINIMUM TEMPERATURE: *40°F*
BLOOMING SEASON: *summer*
OUTSIDE HARDINESS ZONE: *zone 8 and higher*

SOIL: *any well-drained potting mix*
FERTILIZER: *low to moderate amounts of fertilizer; grow tight in a pot*
BEST TIME TO PRUNE: *no later than winter to ensure flowering; prune anytime growth is excessive*
PESTS OR DISEASE TO WATCH FOR:
- *insects: high susceptibility to white fly; some susceptibility to aphids and mealy bug*
- *foliar disease: none*
- *root disease: none*

UNIQUE CHARACTERISTICS/OTHER GROWING TIPS:

Araujia is a wonderful climber that needs some support. In the summertime, place this fragrant specimen in full sun for maximum blooms. For a short period of time, *Araujia* can withstand outdoor temperatures into the teens. When wintering over, bring *Araujia* inside and cut back foliage and vine to its central core group of stems. It can then be kept cold, at about 40°F, in partial sun conditions.

Araujia is an incredibly sweet smelling plant that has a scent similar to a Hoya. Loved for its ease of culture, its vining nature creates spectacular forms on supports. How could such a pleasing plant get the common name "Cruel Plant"? The name was coined because of its relationship to pollinating insects. The plant literally traps and holds any nocturnal insect through the night until dawn, with the insect usually dying. The insect's "cruel" death is where the plant gets its name.

Araujia is a fast grower and does well with support. Encourage vines to wrap around a trellis, stake, or hoop in a container. When planted outside, encourage the vines to wrap around wrought iron structures or fences. We recommend planting *Araujia* in poor soil, or in container culture restricting the nutrients, which will then cause the plant to flower profusely.

the plants

Aristolochia

A floral form that evokes interest and curiosity, compelling the observer to look closer.

BOTANICAL NAME: *Aristolochia*
(a-ris-to-lok´-ee-a)
FAMILY NAME: *Aristolochiaceae*
COMMON NAME: *Dutchman's Pipe,
Pelican Flower*
ORIGIN: *New World Tropics, Brazil,
Costa Rica*

LIGHT: *full to partial sun*
Size and growth: *1 1/2 - 4 feet on
stake or trellis in a container*
MINIMUM TEMPERATURE: *60°F*
BLOOMING SEASON: *spring to fall,
or sporadic blooming depending
on the light level and temperature;
with increased light and warmer
temperatures, Aristolochias can
bloom year-round*
OUTSIDE HARDINESS ZONE: *zone
10 and higher; A. elegans zone 9
and higher*
SOIL: *any well-drained potting mix*
FERTILIZER: *moderate to low
amounts of fertilizer year-round as
long as light levels are high and
temperatures are warm*
BEST TIME TO PRUNE: *early spring
or anytime growth is excessive*

PESTS OR DISEASE TO WATCH FOR:
- *insects: some susceptibility to
mealy bug, but resistant to most
insects; A. grandiflora has some
susceptibility to spider mite; A.
peruviana has some susceptibility
to aphids*
- *foliar disease: none*
- *root disease: A. peruviana is
susceptible*

**UNIQUE CHARACTERISTICS/
GROWING TIPS:**
In general, if the temperature drops
below 60°F for extended periods,
the cold will put *Aristolochia* into a
semi-dormancy. In their native
land, *Aristolochia* are considered to
be tropical weeds. They can literally grow anywhere; therefore, do
not use excessive fertilizer for it
will inhibit flowering. The pollination mechanism is fascinating and
only works because of the unique
flower structure. *Aristolochia grandiflora* gives off the scent of rotting
meat, which attracts flies. A fly
goes into the tube and chamber,
and then bangs around inside, try-
ing to get out, thus pollinating the

Aristolochia gigantea 'Braziliensis'

plant. Note: The odor can become
intense and the flowers are best
enjoyed at a distance.

"Outrageous," "exotic," "botanical wonders," are just a few of the
words used to describe this genus.
Aristolochias have long been
admired for their unique structure,
color and outlandish size. The five
varieties grown at Logee's are the
most unusual of their kind. Their

aristolochia

Left: Aristolochia grandiflora; above: Aristolochia peruviana

climbing ability is astounding, even though they have a heavy vine to support the large flowers.

Recently, we re-introduced *Aristolochia gigantea* 'Braziliensis' to our collection. The flower is over ten inches long and boasts an intricate pattern of white and mottled reddish-brown with a golden yellow center. Surprisingly enough, unlike other *Aristolochias*, this one gives off a fresh, wake-me-up, lemon scent. Although wonderful to have in the home, be forewarned that this Dutchman's Pipe can be tricky to propagate. However, once established, 'Braziliensis' does as well as the others.

Another Dutchman's Pipe worth noting is *Aristolochia peruviana*. The unique clustering of rich, butter-yellow flowers, silhouetted by its chocolate mottled throat, continues to capture gardener's attention everywhere. Of all the *Aristolochias*, this is the most challenging one to grow because of its susceptibility to root disease.

All *Aristolochia* are vigorous growers and do best on some type of support. A trellis or stake lends to container culture. However, they also make nice baskets as long as the vine is trained or encouraged to wrap around the pot. *A. gigantea* 'Braziliensis' and *A. grandiflora* are the largest growing species and need the most room for optimum growth. As a whole, the genus, when given space, will create a mini tropical jungle.

the plants

Begonia
Fibrous Begonia

The flowers, like clusters of jewels, accent the everlasting beauty that is found within the matrix of life.

BOTANICAL NAME: *Fibrous Begonia*
COMMON NAME: *Begonia*
FAMILY NAME: *Begoniaceae*
ORIGIN: *New World Tropics*

LIGHT: *full to partial sun*
SIZE AND GROWTH: *1 - 3 feet in container; cane upright growers*
MINIMUM TEMPERATURE: *60°F; many will tolerate temperatures down into the fifties but not for an extended period of time*
BLOOMING SEASON: *spring, summer, and fall with a few varieties that flower throughout the year*
OUTSIDE HARDINESS ZONE: *zone 10 and higher*
SOIL: *loose potting mix*
FERTILIZER: *moderate amounts of fertilizer when light levels are high; low amounts of fertilizer under shady conditions*
BEST TIME TO PRUNE: *mid to late winter to insure flowering; may prune anytime growth is excessive*
PESTS OR DISEASE TO WATCH FOR:
• *insects: some susceptibility to mealy bug*
• *foliar disease: stagnant air or changes in the temperature can cause mildew; Begonias are especially susceptible during the change of seasons; high humidity can cause botrytis or leaf spots*
• *root disease: none when grown on the dry side*

UNIQUE CHARACTERISTICS/OTHER GROWING TIPS:
Fibrous Begonias are especially noted for their flowers. Grow on the dry side and keep in clay pots and they will thrive. Tolerant to low light, but when given higher light levels, their foliage will become rich, healthy, and more attractive. Begonias bloom under high light and longer days. Light levels also effect fertilizer needs. An increase in light level means more active growth; therefore, more fertilizer is needed. Periodic, severe pruning is also a good idea. Cut Begonias back six to eight inches from the soil. This will create multiple stems giving a thicker, fuller appearance. Prune just above the dormant eyes or growing buds. In culturing begonias, keep growing conditions so foliar disease is minimized. Use preventative spraying. See chapter on disease and troubleshooting for other hints.

Begonia 'My Special Angel'

begonia

Left: B. 'Bubbles'; above: B. 'Kismet'

B. 'Richmondensis' is a fast grower, which makes it a wonderful bedding plant or outdoor container candidate. B. 'Hot Tamale' is an upright grower with long narrow leaves and flowers boasting bright red blooms. B. 'My Special Angel' not only has a great name, but also makes a great basket plant with its speckled leaves and pink flowers. B. 'Bubbles' is a year-round reliable bloomer, and when placed in sunlight, exudes a sweet fragrance. B. 'Kismet' is a perfect windowsill plant because of its miniature size and stunning foliage.

In the plant kingdom, no other family gives such a tremendous show of texture, colors, patterns, and shapes. Whether small specimens that fit on a windowsill, or five-foot "trees," Begonias delight the senses. The flower colors range from bright reds and oranges, to pinks, salmons and whites. Yet, most Begonias are loved for their incredible leaves. As one visitor said, while standing in the middle of the Begonia Greenhouse, "It's as if an artist came through and used the richest colors and most unique shapes and then painted dots, stripes and swirls to intensify the effect."

Begonias, in general, are easy to grow and are very resilient. For the past 75 years at Logee's, we have been known for our Begonias and offer a wide selection. Several different types of Fibrous Begonias exist. The most favored ones are the angel wing type and the hirsute or "hairy-leaved" type.

the plants

B. 'Hot Tamale'

B. 'Connie Boswell'

The Angel Wing Begonias, as the name implies, have leaves that are shaped like celestial wings. 'Sophie's Cecile' is an angel wing that captures the heart and soul with its spectacular beauty. 'San Miguel' is a hairy-leaved Begonia and is not only attractive, but is an extremely resilient grower. When it comes to culture, most of the Fibrous Begonias like a little neglect. Give Begonias a little light in an east, west, or south window and they will thrive.

25

Begonia
Rex Begonia

The patterns and colors bring forth the richness and depth of creation.

COMMON NAME: *Rex Begonia*
FAMILY NAME: *Begoniaceae*
ORIGIN: *Northern India*

LIGHT: *full sun to shade*
SIZE AND GROWTH: *6 - 14 inches in container; most have upright growth habit*

Begonia 'Chocolate Cream'

MINIMUM TEMPERATURE: *60° - 65°F*
BLOOMING SEASON: *not grown for their flowers; the ones that do bloom will flower on and off year-round except in the dead of winter*
OUTSIDE HARDINESS ZONE: *zone 10 and higher*
SOIL: *loose potting mix*
FERTILIZER: *moderate levels of fertilizer when light levels are high*
BEST TIME TO PRUNE: *prune mature rhizomes every couple of years; rexes don't need a lot of pruning*
PESTS OR DISEASE TO WATCH FOR:
- *insects: none*
- *foliar disease: mildew, leaf spots and botrytus*
- *root disease: if grown under damp soil conditions*

UNIQUE CHARACTERISTICS/OTHER GROWING TIPS:

The brilliance of color is unsurpassed in Rexes. Their young leaves are bright and display a fresh intensity of color. The color intensity fades when leaves mature in the summertime and then again when light levels begin to decrease. A variation in leaf color will always be present because of different degrees of light levels. An increase in light level means more active growth; therefore, add more fertilizer.

PLEASE NOTE: Rex Begonias often stop growing in the winter and go into a semi-dormancy. They may drop some leaves, but this is normal. Continue to water and in a few weeks, new growth will begin.

Grow Begonias in clay pots to minimize root rot. Do not over water. Bring them into a slight wilt. For foliar disease, we recommend preventative spraying. To make full specimens, prune tips of growing rhizomes. This will also help maintain form and container size. Some Rexes are dwarf and grow six inches in height, which is ideal for limited space, light gardens, or terrariums.

Rex Begonia leaves are the most unique and colorful found in the Begonia family. Whether the

Left: B. 'Curly Fireflush'; above: B. 'Merry Christmas'; above: ; below: B. 'Lalomie'

spiraled leaves of B. 'Comtesse Louise Erdody', B. 'LaLomie' or B. 'Green Gold', or the distinctive patterning of B. 'Curly Fire Flush', Rexes have been the mainstay for both indoor and outdoor garden design.

Joy Logee Martin has been growing Begonias in her bay window for the past 50 years. They are as much a part of history as her Victorian heirlooms. And when our children visit "Grandma," they immediately play hide-and-seek behind the mature, colorful leaves of the begonias in the bay window.

Rex Begonias are resilient, hardy, and like to be dried out between waterings. They even do well with a slight wilt. Of the 13 greenhouses at Logees, the Begonia House is the last to be watered. With a little bit of fertilizer and slight neglect to watering, Rexes will grow extraordinary leaves and bring design, texture, and pleasure to any living space.

begonia

Begonia
Rhizomatous Begonia

Form, shape, and the richnes of texture are all appealing to the eye.

BOTANICAL NAME: *Rhizomatous Begonia*
FAMILY NAME: *Begoniaceae*
ORIGIN: *New and Old World Tropics*

LIGHT: *full to partial sun*
SIZE AND GROWTH: *6 - 24 inches*

Begonia 'Madame Queen'

in container; upright growth habit
MINIMUM TERMPERATURE: *60°F; will tolerate dips into the fifties*
BLOOMING SEASON: *late winter, early spring; sensitive to day length*
OUTSIDE HARDINESS ZONE: *zone 10 and higher*
SOIL: *loose, well-drained potting mix; air must get into the soil*
FERTILIZER: *moderate amounts of fertilizer; decrease levels when light levels decrease*
BEST TIME TO PRUNE: *after flowering cycle; prune in summer months if growth becomes excessive*
PESTS OR DISEASE TO WATCH FOR:
- *insects: some susceptibility to mealy bug*
- *foliar disease: not as sensitive to mildew as Fibrous and Rex begonias*
- *root disease: grow on the dry side, otherwise can have trouble with root rot*

UNIQUE CHARACTERISTICS/OTHER GROWING TIPS:
Rhizomatous Begonias are not as bright as Rex Begonias. The colors are more subdued but compensated by their wonderful leaf structure. Remember to use a loose potting mix to allow air to get into the root system to avoid root disease. As for fertilization, an increase in light level means more active growth; therefore, add more fertilizer. Overall, Rhizomatous Begonias are known to be resilient growers that are tolerant to the home environment. Amazingly enough, these plants can look their best under shady conditions too. We have one greenhouse at Logee's solely dedicated to Begonias, appropriately called the "Begonia House." In the wintertime, dozens of mature Rhizomatous Begonias are in full bloom. Long flower stems dangling with white and pink blooms are a spectacular sight to see.

From 'Marma Duke', a large Rhizome Begonia, to the dwarf 'Boweriae' (the "Eye Lash" Begonia), Rhizomatous offer different sizes, colors, and form. They are grown for their fascinating foliage and their late winter and

the plants

Left: B. 'Marma Duke'; *above: B.* 'Bowkit'; *below: B.* 'Glaziovii'

early spring blooms. Tall sprays of flowers gracefully rise above their outstanding leaves. Since they can tolerate some shade, they are perfect for an east or west window, leaving the southern exposure for those plants that must capture high light conditions.

Some favorites, all with dramatically different leaves, are *B.* 'Glaziovii' with its rich green, coarse texture; *B.* 'Sweet Magic' with its spiraled, convolutions; and *B.* 'Oliver Twist' and *B.* 'Bunchii', which boast ruffled leaves. For those with limited growing space, try a dwarf variety like *B.* 'Lime Swirl'. For those wanting to experiment with terrariums, the miniature variety *B. prismatocarpa* is popular.

begonia

Bougainvillea

Radiating strength comes from the richness of colors that bring brilliance and presence to the garden.

BOTANICAL NAME: *Bougainvillea*
FAMILY NAME: *Nyctaginaceae*
COMMON NAME: *Bougainvillea*
ORIGIN: *Tropical and sub-tropical South America*

LIGHT: *full sun*
SIZE AND GROWTH: *2 - 3 feet in container; vining growth habit*
MINIMUM TEMPERATURE: *40°F; keep at 60°F for year-round flowering*
BLOOMING SEASON: *year-round in warm temperatures and high light*
OUTSIDE HARDINESS ZONE: *zone 9 and higher*
SOIL: *any well-drained potting mix*
FERTILIZER: *moderate amounts of fertilizer year-round, as long as nighttime temperatures are above 60°F*
BEST TIME TO PRUNE: *prune severely in late winter, if needed, just after a heavy flowering cycle, or selectively prune anytime growth is excessive. These plants take well to severe pruning and can be cut back to the old wood.*

PESTS OR DISEASE TO WATCH FOR:
- *insects: some susceptibility to mealy bug*
- *foliar disease: none*
- *root disease: strong root system*

UNIQUE CHARACTERISTICS/OTHER GROWING TIPS:
Bougainvilleas are resistant to drought and dryness. Variegated varieties are slower growers because of the reduction in chlorophyll on the leaf surface. Most *bougainvilleas* bloom freely year-round except in the winter. They respond to the changes in day length, which initiates a surge of bloom. To encourage flowering, bring *Bougainvilleas* to a slight wilt between waterings. Different varieties have unique characteristics. For example, 'Blueberry Ice' has small-variegated leaves, prolific blooms, and a compact growth habit, which makes an excellent basket. Other varieties that have heavier vines but make wonderful basket plants are 'Thimba', 'Crimson Lake', and 'Barbara Karst'.

If you're looking for standard culture, try the variety 'Raspberry Ice'. Its straight stem, vigorous growth, and bushy, cascading habit are perfect for standard culture.

To winter over, keep *Bougainvilleas* in above-freezing cold spots, such as attic or basement windows. Once exposed to dryness and cold, *Bougainvilleas* will go into a semi-dormancy. The leaves may turn yellow and defoliate. With increased day length and warmth, they will soon come into their first flowering cycle in abundance. Note: the double varieties have to be deadheaded (removal of spent blooms) because the bracts hold onto the vine.

The bract, not the flower, has attracted horticulturists and lay people around the world to grow the genus *Bougainvillea*. At Logee's, we grow over 20 varieties that continue to astound people with their crepe-paper-like flowers, brilliantly colored bracts, and long periods of bloom.

Bougainvilleas are popular not

Bougainvillea 'Delta Dawn'

only for their spectacular colors, but also for their foliage and form. Some varieties such as *B.* 'Delta Dawn' and *B.* 'Orange Ice' boast variegated foliage. The mottled leaves of cream and green intensify the already brilliant colors. Another unique variety, called *B.* 'Thimba', not only has variegated foliage but also has two-shades of bloom — pure white bracts growing beside deep rich magenta bracts.

Bougainvilleas are also known for their versatility of culture. In the south, *Bougainvilleas* are planted directly into the ground, yet in northern climates they do wonderfully in pots. Their straight stems and cascading habit make them a prime candidate for standard culture. And once created, the show-stopping specimen will have guests walking away in awe.

At the greenhouses, we have individual *Bougainvilleas* that bloom for many years. Why? Because we selectively prune the leads, give high light levels, and dry the plants out between water-ings. And since *Bougainvilleas* always flower on the tips, we are able to keep the flowers and still manage the plant, making an attractive specimen. Eventually, these specimens need a hard pruning. We sacrifice the blooms for a short time to re-structure the plant, allowing it to come back into its full glory.

Bougainvillea 'Thimba'

bougainvillea

Bouvardia

The intense fragrance that permeates the evening air carries one to a new level of sensual awareness.

BOTANICAL NAME: *Bouvardia* (boo-var´-dee-ya)
COMMON NAME: *Bouvardia*
FAMILY NAME: *Rubiaceae*
ORIGIN: *Mexico*

LIGHT: *full sun*
SIZE AND GROWTH: *1 1/2 - 3 feet in container; upright growth habit*
MINIMUM TEMPERATURE: *55 °F or 60 °F for wintertime blooms*
BLOOMING SEASON: *everbloomer; intermittent for B. Longiflora with a surge in spring and another surge in the fall*
OUTSIDE HARDINESS ZONE: *zone 9 and higher*
SOIL: *any well-drained potting mix*
FERTILIZER: *moderate amounts of fertilizer year-round as long as temperatures are warm and growth active*
BEST TIME TO PRUNE:
  • *B. ternifolia: anytime — cut back hard during spring to fall when growth is going at full tilt*
  • *B. longiflora: late winter or before new growth begins; if need to prune in summertime because growth is excessive, flowering will be delayed because flowers form on the growing tips*

Bouvardia ternifolia

PESTS OR DISEASE TO WATCH FOR:
  • *insects: high susceptibility to white fly; some susceptibility to mealy bug and aphids*
  • *root disease: some susceptibility.*

Bouvardia longiflora

UNIQUE CHARACTERISTICS/OTHER GROWING TIPS:

To minimize root disease, keep the temperatures warm and grow *Bouvardias* in clay pots. We recommend pinching back *B. ternifolia* as a young cutting to create a full specimen. *B. ternifolia* is a wonderful shrubby plant that becomes fuller with each pruning. *B. longiflora* has an upright stalky habit — occasionally prune hard to avoid a rangy or leggy look. Also, do not over water *B. longiflora*. It has greater susceptibility to root disease, especially in the wintertime during its resting period. On a side note, *B. longiflora's* scent is so intense that it only takes one plant to fill a greenhouse with its nighttime fragrance.

These two *Bouvardias* are exceptional flowering plants. *B. ternifolia* is a brilliant everbloomer and has not been out of flower since its arrival in our greenhouses over a decade ago. The only requirement to succeed with ternifolia is full sun. *B. ternifolia* also needs an occasional hard pruning to contain its growth. But don't despair, for it will quickly return to flowering abundance.

The night-scented *Bouvardia longiflora* also holds a prized position in our greenhouses. Its long, white, tubular flowers carry one of the most delightful and sweetly penetrating fragrances ever. With over 1,500 varieties, this is no small statement. Much like the gardenia, you will never forget this scent. The flowers are short-lived, but the clusters keep emerging from the flowering tips.

bouvardia

Brugmansia

The bright, floral presence and intoxicating fragrance of Angel's Trumpets awaken the senses to worlds beyond our knowing.

BOTANICAL NAME: *Brugmansia*
COMMON NAME: *Angel's Trumpet*
FAMILY NAME: *Solanaceae*
ORIGIN: *South America, Andes, Brazil*

Brugmansia 'Charles Grimaldi'

LIGHT: *full sun*
SIZE AND GROWTH: *4 - 6 feet in container; upright growth habit*
MINIMUM TEMPERATURE: *35°F*
BLOOMING SEASON: *spring, summer and fall; in tropical regions year-round bloom*
OUTSIDE HARDINESS ZONE: *zone 8 and higher*
SOIL: *any well-drained potting mix*
FERTILIZER: *moderate to heavy amounts of fertilizer year-round; eliminate fertilizer when wintering over in a dormant state*
BEST TIME TO PRUNE: *anytime growth becomes excessive. Prune within three to four nodes of the original lateral branching. From here, new growth will emerge, giving a fuller appearance. Severe pruning — cut back a few inches from the soil when wintering over.*
PESTS OR DISEASE TO WATCH FOR:
*   *insects: high susceptibility to spidermite and whitefly; some susceptibility to snails or slugs when grown outside*

UNIQUE CHARACTERISTICS/OTHER GROWING TIPS:

Angel's Trumpets are fast growers that need continuous applications of fertilizer when grown in containers. Allow young cuttings to grow upright until lateral branching occurs. Flowering begins when the plant is approximately three to five feet high. Young cuttings will bloom in four to five months under optimum conditions. Once growth becomes excessive, then prune within three to four nodes of the original lateral branching. This creates a tree-like structure. Angel's Trumpets are especially admired when grown in a standard or tree form. When grown outside, pay attention to the snails and slugs. They may chew a few leaves but this does not effect the overall integrity of the plant. Late in the season, caterpillars may be present. See chapter on Insects and Disease for treatment. Another growing tip — as Angel's Trumpets grow, they demand more water. Keep a close eye on wilt stress.

the plants

Above: Brugmansia x insignis 'Pink'; *upper right: Brugmansia* 'Cypress Gardens'; *lower right: Brugmansia* 'Jean Pasco'

There is no greater gift than the fragrance and form that these magnificent beauties bring to any living space. Angel's Trumpets are especially spectacular when highlighted in a large clay pot and placed outside on a deck or patio. We have also planted six or seven varieties into the ground in early spring. By the end of the summer, we have literally created traffic jams. Interested motorists stop their vehicles to observe the breathtaking wonder of so many flowers cascading from these now five-foot trees.

At Logee's, we grow seventeen

brugmansia

Above: Brugmansia **'Peaches and Cream'**

varieties of angel's trumpets and the flower size ranges anywhere from twelve to twenty-four inches in length with an open face of six to eight inches, often with fluted or curled petals. The colors range from white, yellow, orange, and pink, while the flower color intensifies with age. The blooms last three to five days depending on temperature and humidity. Cooler temperatures will keep the bloom longer. Another attraction these magical plants offer is their inviting fragrance that intensifies when the sun goes down.

WINTERING OVER: After the outdoor growing season, there are several approaches to wintering over the trumpets. First, prune all the limbs or branches on the mature plant. Pruning removes the foliage and prevents leaf drop. Also, pruning gets rid of insects that are most likely lurking on the foliage. Second, bring the now-pruned specimen inside and place in a sunny window. Third, stop or reduce fertilization to limit growth. However, if space is not a problem, then continue to feed the trumpets and they will soon re-flower inside.

Another way to winter over Angel's Trumpets is to bring the un-pruned specimen inside and place in a cool spot without light. Then, the plant will drop all its foliage and remain dormant until spring. Check on it weekly and keep the soil from drying out severely. The temperature should not fall below 32°. In early spring, growth will resume. If the plant has received no light during this time, the foliage will be white. Simply move into a sunny spot to turn foliage green and await the glorious blooms that will burst forth with vigor.

PLEASE NOTE: The juices or sap of the plant are poisonous and ingestion of the plant is discouraged.

the plants

Brunfelsia

The glorious gift of Brunfelsia is the captivating presence of its fragrance and floral form.

BOTANICAL NAME: *Brunfelsia* (brun-fel´-see-a)
FAMILY NAME: *Solanaceae*
COMMON NAME:
* *White flowers: Lady of the Night*
* *Purple flowers: Yesterday, Today And Tomorrow*
ORIGIN: *Tropical Americas*

LIGHT: *full to partial sun*
SIZE AND GROWTH: *2 - 3 feet in container; upright growth habit*
MINIMUM TEMPERATURE: *50°F for most varieties; 60°F for Brunfelsia jamaicensis*
BLOOMING SEASON: *B. 'Australis' blooms intermittently with heaviest bloom during spring; B. jamaicensis blooms intermittently in spring, fall and late winter; B. 'Nitida' blooms intermittently in waves from spring to fall; B. 'Pauciflora Macrantha' is an everbloomer*
OUTSIDE HARDINESS ZONE: *zone 10 and higher*
SOIL: *any well-drained potting mix; need soil between 5.5 - 6.2 pH*
FERTILIZER: *moderate amounts of fertilizer during active growth; can get iron chlorosis problems (treat with chelated iron)*
BEST TIME TO PRUNE: *after the flowering cycle is complete for heaviest flowering and to encourage woody growth*
PESTS OR DISEASE TO WATCH FOR:
* *insects: B. 'Australis' has some susceptibility to white fly; all varieties are susceptible to mealy bug*
* *Brunfelsias are free of disease.*

UNIQUE CHARACTERISTICS/OTHER GROWING TIPS:

B. 'Nitida' sometimes has an objectionable spicy smell to it and blooms intermittently from spring to fall. Grow B. 'Nitida' from seed rather than a cutting. This will make it a stronger specimen with better form. The trick to flowering *Brunsfelsias* is to allow them to become woody. Woody growth is a result of the specimen being grown tight in a pot, restricting water, and fertilizing only when actively growing. Once a mature, free-flowering plant is achieved, you can maintain height by pruning or removing only the top leads of growth. Periodic removal of leads on all varieties will enhance free flowering. B. *pauciflora* 'Macrantha' tends to get loose and rangy looking; therefore, pinch this variety back several times when it is young. Once B. 'Nitida' flowers, we don't prune it very often, only to maintain size. B. 'Australis' is another variety that only needs size maintenance once the stems become woody. B. *jamaicensis* sends up long

Brunfelsia pauciflora 'Macrantha'

Brunfelsia 'Nitida'

shoots. These leads often die back and must be removed to maintain its form. Remember, for this variety, blooms form along the stem at the leaf axis. Encouraging these upright canes will enhance the overall appearance of the flowering specimen.

Grown for their fragrance and flowers, *Brunfelsias* are showy shrubs. As a whole, the genus tends to spring forth in waves of bloom throughout the year. Some varieties are noted for their particular scent. Once they get into mature woody growth, *Brunsfelsias* will last for decades, becoming fuller with age. Whether the sweet reminiscent smell of 'Australis', also known as "Yesterday, Today and Tomorrow," or the fragrant, long, white tubular flowers of 'Nitida', they make great container plants for the windowsill, sunroom, or greenhouse conservatory.

B. 'Australis' is our oldest variety. The original plant has graced our greenhouses for over 100 years. An elderly woman who wanted her beloved houseplant to have a good home gave us this gift. Although an easy grower, with fragrant blue-violet flowers blooming from

Brunfelsia jamaicensis

spring to fall, B. 'Australis' is still not freely cultivated.

B. *jamaicensis*, an endangered species native to the Blue Mountains of Jamaica, is one of the largest white varieties of *Brunsfelsias*.

However, it is challenging to grow because of cane or stem die back. When successfully grown, its intense fragrance permeates the senses.

brunfelsia

39

Burbidgea

Like torches of brilliant light, the blooms spring forth ablaze with the fire of life.

BOTANICAL NAME: *Burbidgea scheizochelia (ber-bid´-jee-a)*
COMMON NAME: *Golden Brush*
FAMILY NAME: *Zingiberaceae*
ORIGIN: *Malayasia and Borneo*

LIGHT: *partial sun*
SIZE AND GROWTH: *1 - 1½ feet in container; upright growth habit.*
MINIMUM TEMPERATURE: *60°F*
BLOOMING SEASON: *twice a year, early summer and late December; sometimes intermittent blooms throughout the year*
OUTSIDE HARDINESS ZONE: *zone 10 and higher*
SOIL: *any well-drained potting mix*
FERTILIZER: *moderate amounts of fertilizer under moderate sunlight conditions; increase amounts of fertilizer when in rapid growth phase during the spring, summer and fall*
BEST TIME TO PRUNE: *do not prune this plant; when plants get too large, divide them; division can be done at any time*

PESTS OR DISEASE TO WATCH FOR:
  insects: some susceptibility to mealy bug
- *foliar disease: none*
- *root disease: none*

UNIQUE CHARACTERISTICS/OTHER GROWING TIPS:
Burbidgeas reproduce by division or by seed. Seeds freely form in the old flower clusters. *Burbidgeas* are self-pollinating. Simply plant the seeds and watch them grow. Don't expose *Burbidgeas* to long, intense periods of heat. They do better under moderate temperatures. They grow from rhizomes, and the shoots multiply quickly making up new foliage. If the foliage looks poor on the old stems, cut them off to the base of the rhizome. This will freshen the overall appearance of the plant. *Burbidgeas* have two heavy flowering cycles, which make them a perfect choice for indoor and outdoor gardening. When in full bloom, specimens display eye-catching splendor.

During the darkest times of the year, these orange flowers spring forth in brilliant clusters. The blooms last two weeks and add wonderful indoor color during the winter holidays. *Burbidgeas* are dwarf gingers and make superb potted plants. They are also loved for their ability to thrive in a home environment and give multiple flowerings throughout the year. Relatively new at Logee's, *Burbidgeas* have amazing strength, vigor, and resiliency to pests and disease.

the plants

Burbidgea scheizochelia

Calliandra

The mesmerizing affect of these tropical wonders intrigues the beholder, opening the heart to joy.

Calliandra surinamensis

BOTANICAL NAME: *Calliandra* (cal-lee-an´-dra)
COMMON NAME: *Pink Powder Puff or Red Powder Puff*
FAMILY NAME: *Leguminosae*
ORIGIN: *Honduras, South Mexico*

LIGHT: *full to partial sun*
SIZE AND GROWTH: *1½ - 4 feet in container; upright growth habit; low growing diffuse shrub*

MINIMUM TEMPERATURE: *40°F*
BLOOMING SEASON: *C. emarginata and C. surinamensis are everbloomers; C. haematocephala blooms November to March*
OUTSIDE HARDINESS ZONE: *zone 10 and higher*
SOIL: *any well-drained potting mix*
FERTILIZER: *moderate to low amounts of fertilizer on a continuous basis; continue through the wintertime as long as the temperatures are above 60°F*
BEST TIME TO PRUNE: *anytime of the year, especially when growth is excessive; flowering will slow down after pruning. C. haematocephala should be pruned from March to September.*
PESTS OR DISEASE TO WATCH FOR:
• *insects: high susceptibility to aphids and mealy bug*
• *foliar disease: none*
• *root disease: none.*

UNIQUE CHARACTERISTICS/OTHER GROWING TIPS:
Calliandras make great houseplants for sunlit windows. They do well in a south, southwest or southeast exposure. Their stems grow outward, and flowers form on the new growth. To give *Calliandras* a full, bushy appearance, prune periodically and watch their admiral response. *C. surinamensis* is an everbloomer that needs higher light levels to flower well. If given partial sun, it's a sparse bloomer.

Calliandras are famous for their ability to bloom year-round. They are reliable bloomers that we consistently recommend to those who want continuous color. Although, don't be fooled — color alone is not what intrigues gardeners. Their flower structure, which is in the shape of a "powder puff," has an almost mesmerizing effect upon the beholder. One can hardly resist the inclination to brush a hand over the floral tips, watching the color wave back and forth.

Originally from Honduras and South Mexico, the flowers are short-lived but emerge continuously in its popular pink or red form. Another feature that sets this container plant apart from others is its versatility to be cultured on a win-

above: Calliandra haematocephala;
right: Calliandra emarginata (Pink Powder Puff)

dowsill, reaching mature growths between one and one-half to four feet high.

We had a unique experience with *Calliandras* while plant collecting in Florida. We thought we had stumbled upon a rare miniature variety of *Calliandra emarginata*, or "pink powder puff." However, when we brought it home to the north, this new species was nothing but our reliable *C. emarginata* that we have always known. What happened? Under high light conditions, like those in Florida, the foliage was dwarf and the flowers were deep red. When we brought our prized possession north, into low light conditions, something unexpected happened. The foliage grew larger, which increased the leaf surface. Why? So the plant could take in the necessary amount of light for proper growth. So, by controlling light level, you can change the size of *C. emarginata*. If you want a miniature, increase the light, and if you want large foliage and pink flowers, reduce the light.

calliandra

Camellia

Softness and gentleness amidst showy flowers create a greater expression of possibilities.

BOTANICAL NAME: *Camellia*
FAMILY NAME: *Theaceae*
COMMON NAME: *Camellia*
ORIGIN: *Northern India, Himlayas, Asia- China, Japan, Northern Indonesia*

C. japonica 'Purity'

LIGHT: *partial sun*
SIZE AND GROWTH: *2 - 4 feet; upright shrubs*
MINIMUM TEMPERATURE: *32 °F*
BLOOMING SEASON: *late fall to early winter; blooms into spring-* time with cool nighttime temperatures in the 30° - 40° range.

OUTSIDE HARDINESS ZONE: *zone 8 and higher; sometimes zones 6 - 7 if protected*
SOIL: *any well-drained potting mix; slightly acidic (soil pH between 4.8 - 5.8)*
FERTILIZER: *very low amounts of fertilizer; will burn; slow growing plant*
BEST TIME TO PRUNE: *immediately after flowering; pinch back young cutting to get full and bushy growth later*
PESTS OR DISEASE TO WATCH FOR:
* *insects: no susceptibility to insects*
* *foliar disease: none*
* *root disease: susceptible*

UNIQUE CHARACTERISTICS/OTHER GROWING TIPS:

Caution must be used when applying fertilizer — make sure to use minimal amounts. Do not fertilize on a regular basis or you will run the risk of burning the leaves. For fertilizer, we recommend using cottonseed meal to top dress *Camellias* before their flush of growth in springtime. Another fertilizer amendment we use is one tablespoon of Epsom salt to one gallon of water twice a year. One to two growth spurts per year equals three to five inches of growth. Stop fertilization when *Camellias* are not actively growing. We also recommend growing *Camellias* in clay pots and giving them time to dry out between waterings. However, this is a fine balance. Excessive amounts of dryness will hurt their flowering. Remember, during the wintertime, *Camellias* prefer 30 - 40°F nighttime temperatures. In the wintertime, if *Camellias* are given hot nights, their buds will fall off. In the summertime, give them some light shade. In warmer climates, *Camellias* grow better at higher elevation.

Years ago, the showy flowers of *Camellias* were used for cut flowers and corsages. They often grew in northern climates in cold houses. The *Camellias* in our collection are over 150 years old and were brought to us from a Newport,

Above: C. surinamensis 'Yuletide';
right: C. japonica 'Pearl Maxwell'

Rhode Island estate. One of our cold houses at Logee's is filled with *Camellias* and continues to delight all visitors, especially in the dead of winter.

Camellias are enduring. A few years ago, we went to an abandoned greenhouse in Massachusetts to see if we could use any hardware. We didn't find any operable equipment, but much to our surprise, we found a *Camellia* 'Japonica' bush that had grown to over 12 feet high and had survived three New England winters. Therefore, we can't stress enough how important cool nighttime temperatures are for successful blooming.

Besides the attractive flowers, many species are deliciously fragrant, like *C.* 'Kramer Supreme' or *C. lutchensis* and its hybrids. Although we only grow twelve varieties, there are over 250 species of *Camellias*. The most popular one is *Camellia sinensis*, which is grown commercially for its green and brown teas.

camellia

Left: Camelia japonica 'Kramer Supreme'
Upper Left: Camelia japonica 'Professor Sargaent'

Cantua buxifolia

Cantua

Mysterious and sacred, the cascading branches and flaring red flowers bring vibrancy and joy to the darkest times of the year.

BOTANICAL NAME: *Cantua buxifolia* (kan´-tew-a)

COMMON NAME: *Sacred Flower of the Incas*

FAMILY NAME: *Polemoniaceae*

ORIGIN: *South America, Andes*

LIGHT: *full sun is a must*

SIZE AND GROWTH: *2¹/₂ - 3 feet in container; sprawling shrub growth habit*

MINIMUM TEMPERATURE: *35°F*

BLOOMING SEASON: *winter and spring*

OUTSIDE HARDINESS ZONE: *zone 9 and higher*

SOIL: *any well-drained potting mix*

FERTILIZER: *low to moderate amounts of fertilizer, spring through fall; decrease or stop fertilizing in wintertime*

BEST TIME TO PRUNE: *immediately after flowering to insure next year's flowers*

PESTS OR DISEASE TO WATCH FOR:
- *insects: high susceptibility to spider mite*
- *foliage disease: none*
- *root disease: susceptible when soil is kept wet with long periods of cool temperatures*

UNIQUE CHARACTERISTICS/OTHER GROWING TIPS:

Cantua buxifolia is a reliable bloomer when grown with high light intensity and kept on the dry side. Though they prefer cool nighttime temperatures, *Cantuas* will grow and flower under warm growing conditions. They bud in the fall, which means they respond to the shortening day length. This is called *photoperiodic*. Their 2½-inch tubular flowers that weep and cascade from a basket somewhat resemble fuchsias. The flowering cycle in greenhouse-grown plants involves several prolific bursts of heavy bloom. Beginning in January and finishing in May, with interludes of modest flowering throughout, *Cantua* is never without flowers during this time. As a new set of buds forms and matures, another set is finishing.

Cantua buxifolia is a sprawling shrub that gracefully weeps from a basket or tantalizes the observer when grown as a standard. Buds appear in December, then come into full bloom by February with showy, two-and-one-half inch tubular flowers. Dating back to the civilization of the Incas, these "sacred flowers" come from high elevations where they grow on rocky outcroppings in the blazing, bright sun. They do well with cool nighttime temperatures and need to dry out after watering.

Although considered a challenging plant to grow, we find that if you pay strict attention to watering and light levels, *Cantua* will give a full floral display in the wintertime. What do we mean by "strict attention?" In late summer and early fall, continue giving *Cantua* a cycle of dryness and slight wilt between waterings. Keep the plant in full sun exposure and watch for spider mites. Only prune immediately after flowering and you will have a healthy plant with those "sacred flowers" abundantly blooming.

cantua

Ceropegia

Trailing, climbing and always reaching higher, this unique presence speaks of great beauty and diversity.

BOTANICAL NAME: *Ceropegia*
COMMON NAME: *Parachute Flower*
FAMILY NAME: *Asclepiadaceae*
ORIGIN: *Africa, Old World Tropics, Philippines*

Ceropegia ampiliata

LIGHT: *partial sun*
SIZE AND GROWTH: *2 - 3 inches in container; vining and trailing growth habit*
MINIMUM TEMPERATURE: *40 °F*
BLOOMING SEASON: *summer*
OUTSIDE HARDINESS ZONE: *zone 10 and higher*
SOIL: *any well-drained potting mix*
FERTILIZER: *moderate amounts of fertilizer during active growth (spring and summer); restrict fertilizer in late fall and winter*
BEST TIME TO PRUNE: *late winter before new growth, or anytime growth becomes excessive; Caution: pruning later than winter may result in no flowers the next summer*
PESTS OR DISEASE TO WATCH FOR:
*   *insects: occasional susceptibility to mealy bug*
*   *foliar disease: grow on dry side to prevent*
*   *root disease: grow on dry side to prevent*

UNIQUE CHARACTERISTICS/OTHER GROWING TIPS:

Ceropegias are carefree plants. They are fleshy, succulent growers and cactus-like in their requirements for care. Go on vacation and forget about them; they like to be neglected. We recommend clay pots so they can dry down. If they are grown at cooler temperatures than 40°F, be sure not to over water. *Ceropegias* dangle down and wrap around themselves, displaying a most unusual flower. We sometimes expect to see the flowers take off into flight with their "parachute" form. *C. ampliata* is unique in that it grows on leafless stems. The leaves that do develop are insignificant. *C. linearis woodiv,* or "Rosary Vine," is an old houseplant that has attractive foliage. Its tight growth habit, perfect for hanging baskets, is tolerant to any gardener's care. The flowers are not large and somewhat obscure.

There are over 200 species of *Ceropegias*. At Logee's, we grow four varieties from Africa and have had much success with them. They make great houseplants and are easy to grow. Only partial sun is needed for *Ceropegias*, leaving your sunny spots for those plants that need brighter light.

The Parachute Flower that we grow is a vining climber that sports unusual flowers and foliage. It

Above: Ceropegia sandersonii;
right: Ceropegia linearis

makes an excellent basket plant for
indoor cultivation when the home
environment mimics their native
habitat. For example: those homes
that are humid in the summer and
dry in the winter, much like our
New England climate, will tend to
be more conducive to growing and
blooming *Ceropegias*.

ceropegia

Cestrum

Glorious showy blooms and intense nighttime scents remind us to live passionately with full expression.

BOTANICAL NAME: *Cestrum* (ses´-strum)
COMMON NAME: *Night Blooming Jasmine*
FAMILY NAME: *Solanaceae*
ORIGIN: *Mexico*

Cestrum elegans 'Newellii'

LIGHT: *full sun*
SIZE AND GROWTH: *2 - 5 feet in container; upright shrub*
MINIMUM TEMPERATURE: *40°F*
BLOOMING SEASON:
- *C. elegans 'Newellii' and 'Nocturnum': year-round*
- *C. elegans 'Smithii': winter*
- *C. diurum: summer*

OUTSIDE HARDINESS ZONE: *zone 9 - 10 and higher*
SOIL: *any well-drained potting mix*
FERTILIZER: *moderate amounts of fertilizer year-round*
BEST TIME TO PRUNE: *for optimum floral show, prune winter bloomers in early summer and summer bloomers in late winter; may also prune anytime growth is excessive; responds to severe pruning — cut 8 - 10 inches from the soil*
PESTS OR DISEASE TO WATCH FOR:
- *insects: high susceptibility to white fly; some susceptibility to aphids; under environmental stress, some susceptibility to spider mite*
- *foliar disease: none*
- *root disease: none*

UNIQUE CHARACTERISTICS/OTHER GROWING TIPS:

Cestrums are rapid growers and need steady amounts of fertilizers. *Cestrum elegans* 'Newellii' has the largest and showiest flowers of all the *Cestrums*. An upright shrub that gives floral displays year-round, this *Cestrum* needs a periodic severe pruning to maintain a full, bushy specimen. **PLEASE NOTE:** After a hard pruning, it may take several months before *Cestrums* are back in bloom. In general, all *Cestrums* are upright growers and need height to bloom. They only flower on the branches or canes that have matured. *C. elegans* "Smithii' is day-length sensitive and needs special attention to the timeliness of pruning. It is best not to prune after early summer to insure bud formation.

Cestrums are grown for their outstanding floral form and intoxicating fragrance. *Cestrum elegans* 'Newellii', like its name implies, shows off its elegant flowers year-round. The dense clusters of cranberry-red blooms grow upright and are the largest and showiest of all the *Cestrums*.

Another favorite *Cestrum* that we grow at the greenhouses is *Cestrum nocturnum*. Also known as the "Night Blooming Jasmine," this variety mimics and even surpasses the true Jasmines for its intense and romantic fragrance after dark. We grow more than 1,500 varieties of plants at Logee's and *Cestrum nocturnum* is always voted "number one" for its ability to emit evening scents of splendor.

Two other varieties worth mentioning are *C. elegans* 'Smithii' and *C. diurum*. *C. elegans* 'Smithii' is a winter and spring bloomer and boasts clusters of pink flowers. *C. diurum*, like an old-fashioned lollipop, emits a sweet, candy-like scent from its upright clusters of white blooms.

Left: Cestrum diurum
Below: C. nocturnum "Night Blooming Jasmine"

cestrum

Clerodendrum

Diversity of color, form and fragrance encourage the beholder to cherish all that is unique unto itself.

BOTANICAL NAME: *Clerodendrum* (Klier-o-den´-drem)
COMMON NAME: *Butterfly Flower, Fireworks, Glory Bower, Pagoda Flower*
FAMILY NAME: *Verbenaceae*
ORIGIN: *Asia and Africa*

Clerodendrum splendens

LIGHT: *full sun*
SIZE AND GROWTH: *1 1/2 - 4 feet in container; mostly shrub with some vining growth habit*
MINIMUM TEMPERATURE: *range from 35°F - 60°F*
BLOOMING SEASON: *mostly spring through fall, with some winter bloomers*
OUTSIDE HARDINESS ZONE: *zone 9-10 and higher*
SOIL: *any well-drained potting mix*
FERTILIZER: *moderate amounts of fertilizer year-round for the fast growers; restrict fertilizer if grown under cold night winter temperatures*
BEST TIME TO PRUNE: *shrub-type variety: pinch the young cuttings; vining and shrub variety: prune right after flowering cycle or anytime growth becomes excessive; responds vigorously to severe pruning*
PESTS OR DISEASE TO WATCH FOR:
• *insects: high susceptibility to white fly and spider mite; some susceptibility to aphids*
• *foliar disease: none*
• *root disease: none*

UNIQUE CHARACTERISTICS/OTHER GROWING TIPS:

Clerodendrums are vigorous growers that respond well to hard pruning. Colors range from white and pink to red, orange and blue. When planted outdoors, *C. bungei* and *C. quadriloculare* will spread by sucker, which sprout from horizontal roots. For young cuttings in a container, pinch the shrub-type variety, which encourages branching. This will create a multiple-stemmed specimen. Overall, *Clerodendrums* are wonderful flowering plants that like a sunny exposure. Their versatility of bloom, color, and form make this a popular genus from which to choose.

Clerodendrums offer a wide spectrum of wondrous colors and exquisite form. With basic cultural care, they are reliable bloomers. Individually, flowers are small, yet collectively, they appear in large umbells or racemes, creating eye-catching displays. At Logee's, we grow eleven varieties, all with varying degrees of color and growth habit. Some are vining in nature,

the plants

NAME	MIN. TEMP.	GROWTH HABIT	BLOOMING SEASON
C. bungei	35°F	shrub-type	spring-fall
C. manahassae	60°F	shrub	winter, spring
C. philippinum	60°F	shrub	everbloomer
C. qaudriloculare COMMON NAME: *Fireworks*	60°F	shrub	winter
C. species	60°F	shrub	winter, intermittent
C. speciosissimum	60°F	shrub	spring-fall
C. splendens COMMON NAME: *Pagoda Flower*	65°F	vine	winter-spring
C. thompsoniae COMMON NAME: *Glory Bower or Bleeding Hearts*	60°F	vine	spring-summer
C. ugandense COMMON NAME: *Butterfly Flower*	50°F	shrub	spring-fall
C. wallachi	50°F	shrub	fall-winter
C. x speciosum	50°F	vine	everbloomer

while others are shrub-like. However the species present themselves, one thing is certain — the blooms awaken the senses to the endless possibilities of creation.

Below: Clerodendrum ugandense; lower right: Clerodendrum thompsoniae

clerodendrum

Left: Clerodendrum species
Below: Clerodendrum spendens
Bottom right: Clerodendrum
speciosissimum

the plants

Clivia

Like a fire that gives warmth and comfort, this Fire Lily invites one to bask in its orange glow.

BOTANICAL NAME: *Clivia*
(Klie'-vee-a)
COMMON NAME: *Fire Lily*
FAMILY NAME: *Amaryllidaceae*
ORIGIN: *Natal, South Africa*

LIGHT: *partial sun or shade*
SIZE AND GROWTH: *1 1/2 - 2 feet in container; upright growth habit*
MINIMUM TEMPERATURE: *35 °F; not above 60 °F during late fall and early winter*
BLOOMING SEASON: *late winter, early spring*
OUTSIDE HARDINESS ZONE: *zone 10 and higher*
SOIL: *any well-drained potting mix*
FERTILIZER: *moderate amounts of fertilizer from spring through summer, then stop*
BEST TIME TO PRUNE: *divide if plants are too large; don't prune after flowering*
PESTS OR DISEASE TO WATCH FOR:
• *insects: some susceptibility to mealy bug*
• *foliar disease: some susceptibility with high humidity and cold temperatures*
• *root disease: none*

UNIQUE CHARACTERISTICS/OTHER GROWING TIPS:

Clivia miniata is a tough plant that is easy to grow in a home environment. Tips for flowering include: 1) find a cool spot; 2) give a drying out period from November to January; 3) grow tight in a pot; and 4) fertilize only during active growing season, which is after flowering. Since Clivias are semi-epiphytic (meaning they grow with little or no soil on rock outcroppings), it is essential not to over water. We can't stress enough that this semi-epiphytic plant needs a dry dormancy period in late fall and early winter. We recommend restricting water and fertilizer completely. Then, place *Clivias* in an area where nighttime temperatures go into the 40s and 50s. By late January, start watering and the buds will emerge in abundance. There are other varieties grown as container plants including a yellow *Clivia miniata* called *Clivia miniata aurea*. Another species called *Clivia nobilis*, a fall bloomer, has individual flowers

Clivia miniata

that hang down from the upright flower stalk.

The Fire Lily has bright orange flowers that give an impression of the ever-changing and elusive colors of fire. *Clivia miniata* generally blooms in the wintertime, although we have occasionally seen it bloom in summer.

clivia

Costus

These small crepe paper-like flowers are fragile, but emerge with great beauty and strength.

Costus cuspidatus

BOTANICAL NAME: *Costus cuspidatus*
COMMON NAME: *Fiery Costus*
FAMILY NAME: *Zingiberaceae*
ORIGIN: *Brazil, Africa and South America*

LIGHT: *partial sun or shade*
SIZE AND GROWTH: *12 - 14 inches in container; upright grower*
MINIMUM TEMPERATURE: *50°F*
BLOOMING SEASON: *summer and fall*

OUTSIDE HARDINESS ZONE: *zone 9 and higher*
SOIL: *any well-drained potting mix*
FERTILIZER: *moderate amounts of fertilizer year-round; decrease fertilizer during wintertime if nighttime temperatures are below 60°F*
BEST TIME TO PRUNE: *prune old canes or divide plant to give more room in pot for expansion*
PESTS OR DISEASE TO WATCH FOR:
- *insects: some susceptibility to mealy bug*
- *foliar disease: none*
- *root disease: susceptibility under wet conditions in wintertime*

UNIQUE CHARACTERISTICS/OTHER GROWING TIPS:

Cuspidatus is grown for its brilliant orange flowers and its ease of culture. Remember to grow *Cuspidatus* tight in a pot under dry conditions to eliminate susceptibility to root diseases. The flowers only form on mature growth. This variety can be propagated by rhizomes or cuttings. Cuttings can be made from the young growth, leaving a stem node below the soil level. If *Cuspidatus* begins to look ratty with damaged foliage, prune severely. Cut back three inches from the soil, removing all the foliage. *Cuspidatus* will then grow back with a full and healthy look.

The brilliant orange flowers of this Fiery Costus are short-lived and fleeting. Yet don't despair, as the blooms come in waves, delighting the eye of the beholder. The partial sun requirement, small size, and ability to be grown tight in a pot endear this variety to the limited-space gardener.

The crepe paper-like flowers emerge on the upright stem of mature growth and bloom well into early winter. Ease of culture and the plant's rhizomatous nature make *Costus cuspidatus* a favorite for the container gardener.

the plants

56

Crossandra

The full floral presence of Crossandra transforms the ordinary into the extraordinary.

BOTANICAL NAME: *Crossandra* (kros-an´-dra)
COMMON NAME: *Fire Cracker Plant*
FAMILY NAME: *Acanthaceae*
ORIGIN: *South India and Arabia, East African*

LIGHT: *full to partial sun; shade*
SIZE AND GROWTH: *1 - 3 feet in container; upright grower*
MINIMUM TEMPERATURE: *60°F*
BLOOMING SEASON: *everbloomer*
OUTSIDE HARDINESS ZONE: *zone 10 and higher*
SOIL: *any well-drained potting mix*
FERTILIZER: *moderate levels of fertilizer year-round; decrease fertilizer in the wintertime when growth slows*
BEST TIME TO PRUNE: *anytime growth becomes excessive; will sometimes go out of bloom in the wintertime — prune when flowering has stopped*
PESTS OR DISEASE TO WATCH FOR:
• *insects: high susceptibility to white fly; some susceptibility to mealy bug and aphids*
• *foliar disease: none*
• *root disease: none*

UNIQUE CHARACTERISTICS/OTHER GROWING TIPS:

Crossandras are grown for their continuous show of flowers over long periods of time. Flowers' heads hold on long after the show is over. Therefore, spent blooms must be removed by hand, called "deadheading." *Crossandras* are easy to grow and easy to flower. *C. species* is a robust grower and the older specimens give months of continuous bloom. Another variety, *C. pungens*, is also worth noting. It's a dwarf version with bright orange blooms and beautiful fine-lined foliage. The plant never gets over twelve inches in height and is easily maintained under six inches. It is also an everbloomer, which is best propagated by seed. Young plants will begin flowering under two inches in height.

Whether rich, deep yellow or fiery orange, flowers in this family are showy and keep bursting forth with vigor. *Crossandra species* is known as the "Firecracker Plant" not only for its colors, but also for its ability to produce flowers one

Crossandra infundibuliformis

right after another, much like a Grande Finale at a fireworks show.

Crossandra infundibuliformis, called the "Firecracker Flower," is known for its ability to grow under low-light conditions and still produce amazing orange blooms. *Crossandra infundibuliformis* differs from *C. species* in growth habit. *Crossandra infundibuliformis* is a low

crossandra

**Left: *Crossandra* species
"Firecracker Plant"
Below: *Crossandra pungens***

grower, making it a perfect choice for windowsill culture. *C. species'* taller growth requires more room or regular maintenance with pruning. We often recommend *Crossandra infundibuliformis* for creating a standard. Its straight stem, ability to create a crown on top, and bright colors make an adorable specimen. Children love them too.

the plants

Dalechampia

Vibrant pink blooms open into their fullness reminding us of heartfelt love with no limits.

BOTANICAL NAME: *Dalechampia dioscoraoefolia (dale-camp-ee´-a)*
COMMON NAME: *Winged Beauty*
FAMILY NAME: *Euphorbiaceae*
ORIGIN: *Central America*

LIGHT: *full sun*
SIZE AND GROWTH: *1 - 3 feet in container; vining growth habit*
MINIMUM TEMPERATURE: *50°F*
BLOOMING SEASON: *everbloomer*
OUTSIDE HARDINESS ZONE: *zone 10 and higher*
SOIL: *any well-drained potting mix*
FERTILIZER: *moderate amounts of fertilizer during active growing season with nighttime temperatures above 60°F*
BEST TIME TO PRUNE: *anytime growth is excessive; may also selectively remove rambunctious runners*
PESTS OR DISEASE TO WATCH FOR:
• *insects: high susceptibility to spider mite; some susceptibility to white fly and aphids*
• *foliar disease: none*
• *root disease: none.*

UNIQUE CHARACTERISTICS/OTHER GROWING TIPS:

Caution: Do not over-fertilize Winged Beauty. It will grow too fast and produce few blooms. It is an incredibly vigorous vine that can grow as fast as a pole bean. Give it plenty of room, or train and prune it on a regular basis. When we have grown this *Dalechampia* in a large container, giving its roots lots of room combined with lots of fertilizer, it only blooms sparsely. When we grow Winged Beauty tight in a pot with attention to fertilizer, it flowers abundantly.

Winged Beauty is one of the most exciting tropical vines in our collection. It produces violet-pink bracts, which oppose each other in an open flat bloom, often reaching five inches in length. This plant is perfect for the summer gardener who wants a vine to fill a sunny spot on a patio or wall, for its greatest show is in late summer and early fall. However, this everblooming vine, when put in full sun, is also well-suited for indoor culture. We have grown

Dalechampia dioscoraefolia

Dalechampia on trellis, hoop, and stake supports. It's a vigorous grower and needs room to vine and climb. Our visitors don't have to look for the vibrant pink colors of Winged Beauty — it finds them. To say this flower shouts wouldn't be accurate either, but we could say that it sings.

PLEASE NOTE: When handling the vine, the foliage can cause a slight itching and skin irritation that is only momentarily annoying.

dalechampia

Dichorisandra

More than what meets the eye, these royal blue flowers inspire creation on all levels.

Dichorisandra thyrsiflora

BOTANICAL NAME: *Dichorisandra thyrsiflora*
COMMON NAME: *Blue Ginger*
FAMILY NAME: *Commeliaceae*
ORIGIN: *Brazil*

LIGHT: *full to partial sun*
SIZE AND GROWTH: *2 1/2 - 4 feet; upright stems and canes*
MINIMUM TEMPERATURE: *60 °F*
BLOOMS: *fall and early winter*

OUTSIDE HARDINESS ZONE: *zone 9 and higher*
SOIL: *any well-drained potting mix*
FERTILIZER: *moderate amounts of fertilizer throughout active growing season; when buds form on mature growth, decrease or completely stop fertilizer*
BEST TIME TO PRUNE: *only prune once a year in early to late winter soon after flowering; prune hard — cut back 6 - 8 inches from the soil; remove water tubers from the root ball on older specimens*
PESTS OR DISEASE TO WATCH FOR:
• *insects: some susceptibility to mealy bug*
• *foliar disease: none*
• *root disease: none*

UNIQUE CHARACTERISTICS/OTHER GROWING TIPS:
What we like most about *Dichorisandra thyrsiflora* are its dense heads of bluish-purple flowers that bloom when others are going dormant, in October through December. Blue Ginger makes a full statement with its deep royal blooms gracing the tips of its upright stems.

The Blue Ginger is a challenge to flower. One factor is the timing of pruning. Prune only after the flowering cycle. If it is pruned any other time of year, it won't flower. Also, the light levels and fertilizer levels must be consistent. You may give Blue Ginger high phosphate feeds (5-10-5 or 15-30-15) during the spring and summer to help insure flowering in the fall.

A unique aspect of Blue Ginger is its ability to grow water tubers. Older plants can literally be lifted out of the pot by these tubers. On mature plants, pull the tubers off. This does not hurt them. Tubers are part of their survival mechanism and grow as a place to store water and nutrients during a dry season. We culture Blue Ginger in large pots (12-14 inches) because of their propensity to grow tubers.

When close attention is given to light levels, fertilizer and pruning, Blue Ginger is not difficult to grow. With patience and practice, a multiple-stemmed, colorful specimen will reward those cool fall days.

the plants

Epiphyllum

Blooms come out at night and fade with the rising sun; yet within that time of glory, they give everything — fragrance, outrageous size, and spectacular displays.

BOTANICAL NAME: *Epiphyllum* (e-pi-fil´-lum)
COMMON NAME: *Night Blooming Cereus, Orchid Cactus*
FAMILY NAME: *Cactaceae*
ORIGIN: *South Mexico and Honduras*

LIGHT: *partial sun*
SIZE AND GROWTH:
- *E. oxypetalum: 4 - 6 feet in container*
- *E. hybrids: 1 1/2 - 2 feet in container; upright to arching growth habit*

MINIMUM TEMPERATURE: *35°F*
BLOOMING SEASON:
- *E. oxypetalum: late spring through fall*
- *E. hybrids: spring*

OUTSIDE HARDINESS ZONE: *zone 9 and higher*
SOIL: *prefers loose open mix*
FERTILIZER: *low to moderate amounts of fertilizer during spring through fall; stop fertilizer in winter*
BEST TIME TO PRUNE: *selective pruning yields the most flowers; prune unruly leads; if a severe pruning is needed, prune immediately after flowering cycle. Flowers that emerge in the present season come off last year's growth; therefore, after a severe pruning, only a few flowers may appear the following year*

PESTS OR DISEASE TO WATCH FOR:
- *insects: some susceptibility to mealy bug*
- *foliar disease: none*
- *root disease: susceptible to root and stem disease if not kept dry during the winter*

UNIQUE CHARACTERISTICS/OTHER GROWING TIPS:
The growth habit of *E. oxypetalum* requires height and support. The growing shoot rises up one to four feet on mature plants, then the leaves form, and flowers form out of the leaves and pendulate downward. *E. oxypetalum* grows best when given room. Its flowers only last a day. *E. hybrids*' flowers last several days. We recommend growing *Epiphyllums* in clay pots so they can dry down between waterings.

Epiphyllum 'Red'

Their epiphytic nature requires air. Remember, during the winter, grow in a cool spot. A little neglect goes a long way to insure flowering.

Words cannot describe the wonder and beauty of seeing *Epiphyllum oxypetalum*, a basketball-sized, pure white bloom that exudes a heady, intoxicating evening fragrance. At the green-

epiphyllum

Above: Epiphyllum oxypetalum; above right: Epiphyllum 'Pink'

houses, we sometimes see as many as fifteen to twenty blooms at once. The show is magical, but the beauty does not last long. The flowers open when the sun goes down and fade in the early morning hours; however, this epiphyte blooms in waves, so the splendor is repeated throughout the summer months.

Other *Epiphylum* hybrids that are as captivating as *E. oxypetalum* are known as the Orchid Cactus. Their flowers last several days, but don't get as large. However, their display is just as spectacular, especially when grown in a hanging basket.

Many years ago we received a sixteen-inch pot of *Epiphylum* Orchid Cactus late in the season. This immense plant took the strength of two men to lift it. Freezing weather was eminent the night of its arrival so the plant was placed in the 35°F work shed greenhouse. It had plenty of light but was forgotten. The next spring, it was given water and the somewhat shriveled leaves recovered and buds began to form en masse. The flowering cycle was so prolific that you could hardly see the foliage. Today, this incredible floral show is still talked about. The neglected Orchid Cactus became a three-foot ball of red blooms with over one hundred flowers opened simultaneously.

the plants

Eucharis

The pure white petals and golden center reveal a truth: darkness does not exist within the light.

BOTANICAL NAME: *Eucharis amazonica (u-car´-is)*
COMMON NAME: *Amazon Lily*
FAMILY NAME: *Amarylidaceae*
ORIGIN: *Northeast Peru*

LIGHT: *partial sun to shade*
SIZE AND GROWTH: *2 feet in container; upright growth habit*
MINIMUM TEMPERATURE: *55°F*
BLOOMING SEASON: *spring, summer and fall*
OUTSIDE HARDINESS ZONE: *zone 10 and higher*
SOIL: *any well-drained potting mix*
FERTILIZER: *moderate amounts of fertilizer throughout the year; reduce fertilizer in winter*
BEST TIME TO PRUNE: *no need to prune; cut back flowering stem after blooming*
PESTS OR DISEASE TO WATCH FOR:
- *insects: high susceptibility to mealy bug*
- *foliar disease: none*
- *root disease: none*

UNIQUE CHARACTERISTICS/OTHER GROWING TIPS:

Eucharis amazonica like to be grown tight in a pot. They flower better when in cramped quarters. To help induce flowering, restrict water for several weeks after a period of vegetative growth. To propagate, divide and place in a small pot. The best time to divide the plant is in late winter or early spring. We've kept *Eucharis* in pots for years and simply prune off the old leaves. As long as these plants don't sit in water, they have a strong root system and are easy to grow. They grow and flower well, even under shady conditions.

The Amazon Lily boasts pure white flowers on tall stems that cascade over dark green, glossy foliage. Much to our liking, it has a sweet soapy scent that is refreshing and delightful. When grown under moderate light conditions, with attention to fertilization and watering, this Lily will amaze you. At Logee's, we have had the same Lily in the same pot for over thirty years. Many times, it flowers three times in one year. When given a stress-induced period of neglect by restricting water, the Amazon Lily will flower time and again.

Eucharis amazonica

eucharis

63

Euphorbia

The striking contrast of sunshine-yellow centers and fiery-red flowers leaves room for brilliant contradictions.

BOTANICAL NAME: *Euphorbia (ewe-for´-bee-a)*
COMMON NAME: *Scarlet Plume*
FAMILY NAME: *Euphorbiaceae*
ORIGIN: *Mexico, South Africa*

LIGHT: *full to partial sun*
SIZE AND GROWTH: *12 - 24 inches in container; upright growth habit*

Euphorbia fulgens

MINIMUM TEMPERATURE:
- *E. fulgens: 60°F*
- *Other varieties: 40°F*

BLOOMING SEASON:
- *E. fulgens: winter*
- *E. geroldii and E. splendens: everbloomers*

OUTSIDE HARDINESS ZONE: *zone 10 and higher*
SOIL: *any well-drained potting mix*
FERTILIZER: *moderate amounts of fertilizer*
NOTE: *only fertilize enough to make growth green and healthy. Do not over fertilize.*
BEST TIME TO PRUNE: *It is critical to prune E. geroldii and E. splendens in spring and summer during active growth. Prune E. fulgens when flowering cycle is complete; do not prune E. fulgens unless actively growing*
PESTS OR DISEASE TO WATCH FOR:
- *insects: E. fulgens: high susceptibility to white fly; some susceptibility to spider mite. E. geroldii and E. splendens are generally pest and disease free*
- *foliar disease: none*
- *root disease: E. fulgens is extremely susceptible to root rot*

UNIQUE CHARACTERISTICS/OTHER GROWING TIPS:

E. fulgens is an exceptional winter bloomer and is often grown in Europe for cut flowers. However, when grown as a container plant, *E. fulgens* is challenging to grow. *E. fulgens* is closely related to the poinsettia and is extremely susceptible to root diseases. *E. fulgens* will often collapse if pruned when not vigorously growing. Why? When the foliage is removed, *E. fulgens* is unable to take up water. Then the roots sit in damp soil and disease takes over. It is important to grow all *Euphorbias* in clay pots, which gives them quick dry down between waterings. Keep them on the dry side during winter and grow under full sun. *E. geroldii* is an everbloomer that's much easier to grow and adapts well to the home environment.

There are more than 2,000 species in the *Euphorbiaceae* family. *Euphorbias* are diverse in their

Below: Euphorbia spendens;
Right: Euphorbia geroldii

growth habit, from succulents and thorny, to herbaceous soft leafy growth. They shower us with their unusual bloom and form. We grow several *Euphorbias* for their impressive flowers. *E. fulgens*, unusual for a *Euphorbia*, blooms in deep orange-colored clusters. Most impressively, *E. fulgens* flowers during the darkest days of the year. Another *Euphorbia*, *geroldii*, has been coined "The Thornless Crown of Thorns," not only for its blood-red blooms, but also for its distinct similarity in growth to *E. splendens*, which is called "The Crown of Thorns."

E. splendens millii, one of the oldest houseplants, is a dwarf *Euphorbia* that is grown for its ability to grow on a windowsill. Many *Euphorbias* are cactus-like in their ability to survive under tremendous stress, such as low water and moderate light levels. Not only favored as an indoor plant, many *Euphorbias* are popular as landscape plants in arid, warm climates as well.

euphorbia

Felicia

These sky blue fowers bring a rich vibrancy of truth — joy is found in every petal!

BOTANICAL NAME:
Felicia amelloides
COMMON NAME: *Blue Daisy or Kingfisher Daisy*
FAMILY NAME: *Compositae*
ORIGIN: *South Africa*

LIGHT: *full sun*
SIZE AND GROWTH: *1 - 1½ feet in container; upright to sprawling growth habit*
MINIMUM TEMPERATURE: *50°F*
BLOOMING SEASON: *everbloomer, with heaviest flowering in the fall, winter and spring*
OUTSIDE HARDINESS ZONE: *zone 9 and higher*
SOIL: *any well-drained potting mix*
FERTILIZER: *moderate amounts of fertilizer year-round; if grown under cold nights and low light, eliminate fertilizer*
BEST TIME TO PRUNE: *during the summer at lightest flowering cycle*
PESTS OR DISEASE TO WATCH FOR:
• *insects: some susceptibility to white fly; occasional susceptibility to spider mite*
• *foliar disease: none*
• *root disease: susceptible to root rot*

UNIQUE CHARACTERISTICS/OTHER GROWING TIPS:
Critical: *Felicias* must have full

Felicia amelloides 'Astrid Thomas'

Felicia amelloides 'Variegata'

sunlight because they belong to the daisy family. Grow them in clay pots, on the dry side, to keep the stem lengths down and maintain a healthy root system. To prevent root disease, do not grow *Felicias* under damp conditions and high heat, or grow them too wet under cold conditions. To create the best specimen, grow with an occasional wilt. Although they need considerable amounts of water under high-light conditions, the dryness makes them woody and compact, giving a fuller appearance.

"He loves me; he loves me not." Plucking the petals of daisies on a warm afternoon is reminiscent of days gone by. There is nothing quite as whimsical as daisies growing in a pot. The varieties that we grow at Logee's are *Felicia amelloides* 'Astrid Thomas' and *Felicia amelloides* 'Variegata'. Both are a delight to have in the greenhouse and bloom continuously through-out the year. The rich blue petals with their bright yellow centers greet all that pass with a cheery "Hello."

The variegated variety with marbled green and white leaves creates a wonderful background for these most desirable daisies. They make excellent basket plants and have been a favorite for windowsill pot culture for many years. These daisies bloom abundantly during the darkest days of winter.

felicia

Fuchsia

Listen closely, for there is a depth and splendor that emanates from these two-tone bell-shaped blossoms.

BOTANICAL NAME: *Fuchsia (few-sha'-a)*

COMMON NAME: *Fuchsia*

FAMILY NAME: *Onagraceae*

ORIGIN: *New World Tropics, High Elevation*

LIGHT: *shade to partial sun in summer; partial sun to full sun in winter*

SIZE AND GROWTH: *1 - 2 feet; upright to trailing growth habit*

MINIMUM TEMPERATURE: *40°F*

BLOOMING SEASON: *spring through fall*

OUTSIDE HARDINESS ZONE: *zone 9 and higher*

SOIL: *any well-drained potting mix*

FERTILIZER: *moderate amounts of fertilizer throughout the active growing season*

BEST TIME TO PRUNE: *mid to late winter, just before growth starts or when they are coming out of their winter rest. Do not prune in the summer unless plant becomes unsightly.*

PESTS OR DISEASE TO WATCH FOR:
- *insects: highly susceptible to white fly; some susceptibility to spider mite*
- *foliar disease: some susceptibility to foliar disease under high humidity with cool temperatures*
- *root disease: some susceptibility to root rot*

UNIQUE CHARACTERISTICS/OTHER GROWING TIPS:

Fuchsias are not tolerant to high temperatures. Under high heat, *Fuchsias* transpire rapidly. This means they let off water from their leaves faster. Unfortunately, their root system cannot move moisture up from the soil fast enough to keep up with the transpiration rate. This process puts them into a wilt even when the soil is moist. Often, this wilt is interpreted as a plant that needs to be watered. Do not water; they need a drying out period. The most common mistake is over watering. If watered during this time, they are susceptible to root rot and may suddenly collapse. Or if exposed to repeated heat stress, they will eventually defoliate and die. Culture them in a shady spot to help reduce transpiration stress. Undoubtedly, *Fuchsias* are amazingly showy plants and the modern hybrids are large and full with growth habits that are upright as well as cascading.

Huge double-flowers cascading from a basket or a standard tree form are one of the reasons *Fuchsias* are so popular. These showy plants have become a major spring bedding crop in the United States. Over 8,000 cultivars have been recorded with over 2,000 in cultivation today. *Fuchsias* grow rapidly and are easy to culture.

We grow more than twelve varieties. The most popular variety is *Fuchsia* 'Honeysuckle'. This everbloomer is heat tolerant, which is unusual for the genus, and always blooms during the winter holidays. Another variety, less tolerant to heat with a short blooming season, is a lovely dwarf hybrid. *F.* 'Bluette', although not as easy to grow as the others, speaks of softness with its

Above: Fuchsia 'Bluette'; *right: Fuchsia* 'Yeultide'

rose-pink sepals and blue petals.

Fuchsias grow best in moderate climates, such as the Pacific Coast, northern areas of the East Coast, or at high elevations. Cool summers are necessary. They do not tolerate heat well. We have heard that *Fuchsias* do well in southern climates (much like people) as long as an air-conditioned room and moderate light levels are available.

fuscia

Gardenia

The pristine white blossoms and intoxicating fragrance inspire mystery, romance, and passion.

BOTANICAL NAME: *Gardenia* (gar-den´-ee-a)
COMMON NAME: *Gardenia, Cape Jasmine*
FAMILY NAME: *Rubiaceae*
ORIGIN: *East Asia*

LIGHT: *full sun*
SIZE AND GROWTH: *see chart*

Gardenia 'White Gem'

MINIMUM TEMPERATURE: *60°F*
BLOOMING SEASON: *see chart*
OUTSIDE HARDINESS ZONE: *zone 8 and higher*
SOIL: *any well-drained potting mix on the acidic side, with pH levels ranging from 4.5 - 6.2*
FERTILIZER: *low to moderate levels of fertilizer year-round; susceptible to iron chlorosis*
BEST TIME TO PRUNE: *after flowering cycle is complete or during active growth; prune anytime growth is excessive; do not prune during the slow growth of the winter months*
PESTS OR DISEASE TO WATCH FOR:
- *insects: high susceptibility to spider mite (increase humidity to control)*
- *foliar disease: none*
- *root disease: high susceptibility to fungal root rots; grow on the dry side*

UNIQUE CHARACTERISTICS/OTHER GROWING TIPS:

Gardenias are wonderfully fragrant plants with exquisite flower form but can be difficult to grow in pots.

Why? Their susceptibility to spider mite and root diseases. Here are a few tips to minimize their predisposition. First, control the environment. Grow them on the warm side when maintained in pots. This keeps the root system active and causes the plant to use more water, thus bringing the soil to a quicker state of dryness. Second, grow them tight in the pot. We recommend clay pots. Third, mist the foliage under low humidity to reduce spider mite infestation. *Gardenias* are also susceptible to iron chlorosis, which is an interveinal lightening of the leaves. This is caused by an iron deficiency, which can be aggravated by high pH levels. Add chelated iron to the soil and splash it onto the leaves. The leaves and roots readily absorb the chelated iron. Also, the addition of tea water on a monthly or bi-monthly basis will help keep the soil acid.

One other problem with *Gardenias* that we are often asked about is a condition called "bud blast." Bud blast happens when a

G. jasminoides 'Prostrata'; *Gardenia* 'Four Seasons' appears on page 8.

fully-budded, healthy *Gardenia* in the fall is brought into the home environment and suddenly loses all its buds. What happened? Two factors: the daytime and nighttime temperature differential was not enough, and the light levels dropped. What to do? When you bring your plant inside, pinch off all the young growth that is emerging next to the developing bud. This forces all the energy of the plant into the bud, allowing the flower to hold on. Grow in an area where the plant will get full sun exposure and a ten to fifteen degree drop in the nighttime temperatures on a consistent basis.

Gardenias have long been known for their heady, intoxicating fragrance, which inspires mystery, love and passion. Our collection at Logee's has been around as long as we have. Our freest blooming variety is *G. jasminoides* 'Fortuniana' and has been known as the corsage Gardenia for years. Recently, our newest *Gardenia*, called 'Four Seasons', had the prestigious honor of being featured on the front cover of our annual catalogue. And true to its name, pristine, white, fragrant flowers emerge "four seasons" of the year.

One other variety that continues to delight gardeners is *G. jasminoides* 'Prostrata'. Also known as the "Cape Jasmine," this fragrant dwarf variety is well-suited for windowsill culture and maintains a compact stature with ease. However, they are a challenge to grow in containers.

NAME	SIZE	GROWTH HABIT	BLOOMING SEASON
G. 'Belmont'	4 feet	shrub	late winter - summer
G. 'Four Seasons'	1 1/2 - 2 feet	shrub	everbloomer
G. jasminoides 'Fortuniana'	2 1/2 feet	shrub	everbloomer
G. jasminoides 'Prostrata'	< 12 inches	trailing	late winter - spring
G. taitensis	3 feet	shrub	spring - summer
G. 'White Gem'	6 - 8 inches	shrub	late winter - summer

gardenia

Gelsemium sempervirens

Gelsemium

With an expansive nature that climbs and wanders, this Jasmine reminds us to enjoy the richness of life in the present.

BOTANICAL NAME: *Gelsemium sempervirens (gel-sem´-ee-um)*
COMMON NAME: *Carolina Jasmine*
FAMILY NAME: *Loganiaceae*
ORIGIN: *North America, Guatemala*

LIGHT: *full to partial sun*
SIZE AND GROWTH: *1 - 3 feet; vining in habit*
MINIMUM TEMPERATURE: *35°F*
BLOOMING SEASON: *fall, winter and spring*
OUTSIDE HARDINESS ZONE: *zone 8 and higher*
SOIL: *any well-drained potting mix*
FERTILIZER: *low to moderate amounts of fertilizer during active growth; stop feeding during cold months; too much fertilizer can result in burned leaves*
BEST TIME TO PRUNE: *after flowering is complete; the growth of summer produces flowers in the fall and winter; occasionally prune hard, keeping only some foliage and stem*
PESTS OR DISEASE TO WATCH FOR:
- *insects: some susceptibility to mealy bug*
- *foliar disease: Botrytis if grown under cool damp conditions*
- *root disease: none*

UNIQUE CHARACTERISTICS/OTHER GROWING TIPS:
The Carolina Jasmine likes cool nighttime temperatures and will tolerate freezing temperatures. We have heard of cases where Carolina Jasmines were successfully wintered-over outside in zone 7 and the lower edges of zone 6. This slow grower needs one full growing season to make a spectacular basket or trellis plant. When grown in clay pots and dried down between waterings, the flowering cycle for indoor culture continues for a long time.

Gelsemium sempervirens is one of the most under-utilized climbers in horticulture. It's easy to grow, has magnificent fragrant yellow flowers, and is an excellent climber. Bright yellow blooms appear during the darkest days of the year. We let it show off around the greenhouses as it trails and vines on structures. And its baby-powder fragrance continues to delight visitors eight months of the year. Although Carolina Jasmine flowers easily, one good growing season is needed to make a full, outstanding specimen. Interestingly enough, when grown in the wild, Carolina Jasmine only flowers in early spring, but when grown inside in a pot in full sun, blooms can be enjoyed from November to June.

PLEASE NOTE: Poisonous — Do not ingest.

Gelsemium sempervirens

gelsemium

Hardenbergia

The beauty of this lilac vine begins in the darkest days of the year and continues until spring, giving faith and hope for a new beginning.

BOTANICAL NAME: *Hardenbergia violacea*
COMMON NAME: *Lilac Vine*
FAMILY NAME: *Leguminosae*
ORIGIN: *East Australia, Tasmania*

LIGHT: *full sun a must*
SIZE AND GROWTH: *1 - 3 feet in container; vining growth habit*
MINIMUM TEMPERATURE: *35°F*
BLOOMING SEASON: *late winter and early spring*

OUTSIDE HARDINESS ZONE: *zone 9 and higher*
SOIL: *any well-drained potting mix*
FERTILIZER: *moderate levels of fertilizer throughout growing season; stop feed during winter*
BEST TIME TO PRUNE: *immediately after flowering to allow enough growth before next flowering cycle*
PESTS OR DISEASE TO WATCH FOR:
- *insects: some susceptibility to mealy bug*
- *foliar disease: susceptible if high humidity*
- *root disease: susceptible if grown too wet*

UNIQUE CHARACTERISTICS/OTHER GROWING TIPS:
To initiate flower buds, the Lilac Vine needs cool nighttime temperatures, below 60°F, on a regular basis. Buds form in late summer and early fall. Problems in culture arise from low light levels or damp soil. Give it dry conditions and full sun and watch this winter bloomer come into its full glory. Also, this vine prefers to be trained on a support such as a stake or trellis, or cultured in a hanging basket in a sunny window.

This winter-blooming Lilac Vine gives an impressive show of purple-violet flowers. When it first came into our collection, we cultured it in a basket and placed it in a sunny spot. We chose our oldest greenhouse with glass peaked ceilings that are over fifteen feet high. For the first two weeks, the watering crew didn't notice the new addition hanging high in the corner, so it never got watered. The plant went into a wilt and looked like it wouldn't live. We watered the drooping specimen. It perked up. This cycle, by chance, happened several times. The plant was simply forgotten. And one month later, much to our surprise, the Lilac Vine was profusely blooming in its fullness with outrageous pea-shaped flowers.

The moral of the story is simple. Keep the Lilac Vine on the dry side and it will respond with spectacular blooms. In other

words, forget to water it once in a while. Why does it do so well under drought? We were mimicking its native habitat, the scrubland of Australia, where dry periods are a common occurrence.

Hardenbergia violacea

hardenbergia

75

Hibiscus

An expression of joy and brightness reflect an inherent fullness found within every flower.

BOTANICAL NAME: *Hibiscus rosa sinensis*
COMMON NAME: *Hibiscus*
FAMILY NAME: *Malvaceae*
ORIGIN: *Tropical Asia, Hawaii*

Hibiscus 'Edna Bogaert'

LIGHT: *full sun*
SIZE AND GROWTH: *2 - 4 feet in container; upright growth habit*
MINIMUM TEMPERATURE: *60°F*
BLOOMING SEASON: *year-round with high light levels; otherwise, generally spring through fall*
OUTSIDE HARDINESS ZONE: *zone 10 and higher*

SOIL: *any well-drained potting mix*
FERTILIZER: *moderate to high amounts of fertilizer year-round; reduce in the winter*
BEST TIME TO PRUNE: *anytime growth is excessive; severely prune in late winter (may take several months before blooms return)*
PESTS OR DISEASE TO WATCH FOR:
• *insects: high susceptibility to white fly and aphids; some susceptibility to spider mite under dry conditions with high heat*
• *foliar disease: none*
• *root disease: some susceptibility to root rot when temperatures are cool and light levels are low*

UNIQUE CHARACTERISTICS/OTHER GROWING TIPS:
Young plants produce flowers, which have a pale color to their bloom. With mature growth, the flower color will intensify. Although flowers only last one or two days at the most, they are spectacular in their size, color, and form. Different cultivars bloom with different degrees of ease. If plants fail to bloom or are shy bloomers, increase the light level and reduce the nitrogen level in the fertilizer. Only re-pot to accommodate the plant.

We grow *Hibiscus* in the same pot for many years with simple pruning to maintain the sizes. *Hibiscus* do not like extended periods of cold below 60°F. They are heavy feeders and vigorous growers; therefore, remember to give them a continuous supply of fertilizer. Occasionally apply a high phosphate feed, every month to six weeks. They respond well to severe pruning but often will not come back into flower for several months because flowers form on the terminal tips. Grow in clay pots. Bring soil to dryness between waterings, but be cautious of wilt stress.

Tropical flowers and *Hibiscus* are used interchangeably. Native to Hawaii and the south Pacific Islands, *Hibiscus* have long been linked to paradise and there's good reason for them to be. *Hibiscuses* have enchanted gardeners and non-gardeners for centuries. Their intense array of colors, large flower

Hibiscus rosa sinensis 'The Path'

size, and everblooming nature all add to their mystique, much like paradise itself.

We grow over two dozen cultivars that are selections of *rosa sinensis* hybrids. These varieties are broken down into two groups of cultivars. The first are the multi-colored, dinner plate-size flowers that are our specialty. The second group of *Hibiscus* is common in the horticultural trade. They are the easy rooters and growers, which

Hibiscus 'Donna Lynn'

hibiscus

Above: Hibiscus 'Estelle K'; *right: Hibiscus* 'Kona'

produce moderate-size flowers. The first group, although more difficult to propagate and slower to grow, is well worth the wait. *H.* 'Donna Lynn' is especially spectacular for its multi-show of rainbow colors all within one flower. *H.* 'The Path' is popular for its deep pink center that bleeds outward into yellow edges. And we can't forget one of our oldest hybrids, *H.* 'Estelle K', for its neon-orange brilliance. With a little attention to watering and environmental conditions, the pride and pleasure of seeing one of these beauties bloom before your eyes is astounding.

the plants

These blooms create entertainment and excitement as the gardener watches the infinte possibilities of new growth.

BOTANICAL NAME: *Hoya (Hoy´-a)*
COMMON NAME: *Hoya*
FAMILY NAME: *Asclepiadaceae*
ORIGIN: *Tropical Asia*

LIGHT: *partial sun to shade*
SIZE AND GROWTH: *see chart*
MINIMUM TEMPERATURE: *60°F; most will tolerate 55°F*
BLOOMING SEASON: *see chart*
OUTSIDE HARDINESS ZONE: *zone 10 and higher*
SOIL: *loose potting mix; semi-epiphytic in habit; most soil-less mixes work well*
FERTILIZER: *moderate levels of fertilizer during active growth; stop feed when growth has slowed*
BEST TIME TO PRUNE: *immediately after flowering*
PESTS OR DISEASE TO WATCH FOR:
• *insects: some susceptibility to mealy bugs; H. bella is susceptible to spider mites*
• *foliar disease: none*
• *root disease: susceptible to root rot if grown too wet*

UNIQUE CHARACTERISTICS/OTHER GROWING TIPS:

Hoyas are excellent houseplants that are adaptable to dry conditions and low light levels. Prune these slow growing vines only when absolutely necessary. We discourage severe pruning. Do not prune off flowering spurs. The spurs, which are last year's flowering stems, will re-bloom. *H. bella*, and *H. pubera* do not have flowering spurs. *H. bella* flowers easily. Remember, *Hoyas* are epiphytes and like to be dried out. Do not over water. At Logee's, we grow varieties that bloom easily. There are some varieties that come from higher elevations in tropical regions and can be difficult to bloom in home conditions. If you have a high elevation *Hoya*, it is imperative that you give it cool nights during the winter. The *Hoyas* that we grow have fragrant flowers with attractive foliage and do well when trained on a trellis or stake, or placed in a basket.

Hoya lanceolata bella

At Logee's, we grow two dozen varieties of *Hoyas*. They are loved for their fragrance, showy blooms, and interesting foliage. Yet the best reward *Hoyas* give is their ability to adapt to neglectful care. Virtually anyone can grow a *Hoya*. Mother Glass, who is a wonderful woman

hoya

Above: Hoya pubera; lower right: Hoya pubera close up

with 14 grandchildren, has no time for plants. Yet she has successfully grown *Hoyas*. (Not because she tried, but because of circumstance.) Every winter, she and her husband go south. They turn down the heat in the house and never think about asking anyone to water their *Hoya*. Every spring they return and their *Hoya* of twenty years, which has

Hoya archboldiana

NAME	SIZE	GROWTH HABIT	BLOOMING SEASON
H. archboldiana	12 - 24 inches	vining	spring, summer, fall
H. australis	12 - 16 inches	vining	summer
H. carnosa 'Crispa' COMMON NAME: *Hindu Rope Plant*	6 inches	trailing	summer
H. coronaria	10 - 20 inches	vining	summer, fall
H. lacunosa	12 inches	vining	everbloomer
H. lanceolata bella COMMON NAME: *Miniature Wax Plant*	6 inches	scandant	summer
H. lanceolata bella 'Variegata'	6 inches	trailing	summer
H. pubera	10 inches	vining	fall
H. serpens	2 inches	trailing	summer

Hoya coronaria

never been fertilized and lives in a western window, rewards them with a fragrant bloom. What a welcoming tradition — to enjoy fragrant flowers with little effort.

As the story goes, *Hoyas* love a dry down period, and many like cool nighttime temperatures. When there is a dry season during the winter, coupled with low temperatures, *Hoyas* reward the gardener with flower and fragrance.

the plants

The bright fiery colors of this plant never waver year-round, a reminder that the flame of life burns eternal.

BOTANICAL NAME: *Ixora javanica* (iks-or´-a)
COMMON NAME: *Jungle Geranium*
FAMILY NAME: *Rubiaceae*
ORIGIN: *Tropical Asia, Java and Malay Peninsula*

LIGHT: *full or partial sun*
SIZE AND GROWTH: *12 - 18 inches in container; upright growth habit*
MINIMUM TEMPERATURE: *60 °F*
BLOOMING SEASON: *everbloomer*
OUTSIDE HARDINESS ZONE: *zone 10 and higher*
SOIL: *any well-drained potting mix; slightly acidic*
FERTILIZER: *moderate levels of fertilizer throughout the year; susceptible to iron chlorosis — correct by adding chelated iron to fertilizer; best to use a fertilizer that contains trace minerals*
BEST TIME TO PRUNE: *immediately after flowering cycle or anytime growth is excessive; takes well to moderate/severe pruning which thickens the growth*
PESTS OR DISEASE TO WATCH FOR:
• *insects: mealy bug, spider mite, aphids and scale*
• *foliar disease: none*
• *root disease: none*

UNIQUE CHARACTERISTICS/OTHER GROWING TIPS:

Ixora javanica is a showy, everblooming container plant that flowers easily under a variety of light conditions. We use *I. javanica* as a display plant and with little effort, blooms of color fill our greenhouses. Once *I. javanica* has reached maturity, this full and flowering plant is easily maintained.

Over the years, we have grown many different *Ixoras* in pots and containers. Today, we grow *Ixora javanica* because of its showy blooms, strong root system, and reliability to flower year-round. Other varieties in the northern temperate indoor environment have a greater susceptibility to root rots and are not as predictable in their ability to produce flowers.

We also like *I. javanica* for its rapid growth under a variety of light conditions. To our surprise, *I. javanica* is not widely grown in tropical areas. Why? *I. javanica,*

Ixora javanica

unlike other varieties, does not have a stiff upright stem; therefore, when grown out of a pot, the weight of the flower bends the stems to the ground. We often stake young plants to assist the flowers. After several hard prunings, they'll stay up on their own and once mature, will give a continuous show of brilliant orange flowers.

ixora

Jasminum

This intoxicating fragrance is an invitation to know the essence of pure love through the senses.

BOTANICAL NAME: *Jasminum*
COMMON NAME: *Jasmine*
FAMILY NAME: *Oleaceae*
ORIGIN: *Old World Tropics*

Jasminum sambac 'Maid of Orleans'

LIGHT: *full to partial sun*
SIZE AND GROWTH: *see chart*
MINIMUM TEMPERATURE: *see chart*
BLOOMING SEASON: *see chart*
OUTSIDE HARDINESS ZONE:

J. parkeri, J. officinale, J. humile revolutum: zone 8

J. tortuosum: zone 9

all others: zone 10

SOIL: *any well-drained potting mix; slightly acidic*
FERTILIZER: *moderate levels of fertilizer throughout the year as long as temperatures are above 60°F; discontinue feed for varieties grown in cool nights. Susceptible to iron chlorosis; add chelated iron to fertilizer as needed.*
BEST TIME TO PRUNE: *after flowering cycle is complete or when growth is excessive; exception: J. sambac and J. nitidum benefit from periodic pruning to keep them in bush form. J. sambac and J. nitidum flower better in bush form but can be left alone and trained as vines.*
PESTS OR DISEASE TO WATCH FOR:
- *insects: many have high susceptibility to spider mite such as the softer leafed varieties like J. sambac cultivars, J. polyanthum, and J. parkeri*
- *foliar disease: none*
- *root disease: some susceptibility in the J. sambac cultivars*

UNIQUE CHARACTERISTICS/OTHER GROWING TIPS:

Jasmines usually have yellow or white flowers, although there is a pink form called *J. beesianum* and its hybrid *x stephanense*. There are two types of bloomers — the everbloomers and the seasonal bloomers. Seasonal bloomers respond to day length and cold temperatures, which stimulate flowering. *J. polyanthum*, a winter bloomer, needs at least four to six weeks of cool nighttime temperatures to set the buds. *J. rex*, a fall and winter bloomer, also responds to shortening day length. Summer bloomers like *J. angulare* and *J. molle* respond to longer days.

The *J. sambac* varieties have weak root systems. Therefore, when there is growing difficulty, we

Jasminum angulare

recommend grafting *J. sambac* onto other varieties like *J. tortuosum*, which has a strong root system.

Jasmines are known for their fragrance. Within the Jasmine family, there are many different scents. The *sambac* varieties have a rich, heavy scent. *J. volubile* is light and sweet. *J. polyanthum* heavily permeates the air and can easily fill a room with its sometimes overpowering fragrance.

Jasmines are also varied in their growth and vigor. *J. polyanthum* is a rank and vigorous grower. *J. tortuosum*, once established, is a heavy

NAME	SIZE	TEMP	GROWTH HABIT	BLOOMING SEASON
J. angulare	1½ - 2½ feet	40°F	*vine, climber*	*spring, summer, fall*
J. humile revolutum	1 - 2 feet	40°F	*vine, stiff-stemmed*	*everbloomer*
J. molle	1 - 3 feet	50°F	*vine, climber*	*summer and fall*
J. nitidum	1 - 3 feet	50°F	*vine, stiff-stemmed*	*everbloomer*
J. officinale grandiflorum	1 - 3 feet	40°F	*vine, climber*	*spring, summer, fall*
J. parkeri	10 inches	40°F	*shrub, dwarf*	*spring and summer*
J. polyanthum	1 - 3 feet	40°F	*vine, climber*	*winter*
J. rex	1 - 2 feet	60°F	*vine, climber*	*fall, winter*
J. sambac	1 - 3 feet	60°F	*vine, stiff-stemmed*	*everbloomer*
COMMON NAMES: **Arabian Knights, Belle of India, Grand Duke of Tuscany, Maid of Orleans**				
J. volubile	1 - 3 feet	40°F	*vine, climber*	*spring, summer*
J. tortuosum	1 - 3 feet	50°F	*vine, climber*	*spring, summer, fall*

jasmine

Above: Jasminum humile revolutum; right: Jasminum polyanthum

vine that produces vigorous leads and quickly fills a growing area. *J. angulare* is similar in form to *tortuosum* except it is more easily contained. The *sambac* cultivars such as 'Belle of India' and 'Grand Duke' are temperamental, slower growers.

Jasmine has long been considered a flower of romance, love, and sweetness. Its heavy and wonderful fragrance permeates the senses beyond this world. In many cultures, Jasmine is considered sacred. *Jasmine sambac* 'Maid of Orleans' is a variety that's grown throughout Tropical Asia for its intoxicating fragrance and popular use as a cut flower. In keeping with tradition, women in India wear sprigs of Jasmine every evening to attract good tidings.

In the Buddhist tradition, praying with a handmade Jasmine wreath of flowers placed around Buddha's neck is said to bring good fortune to one's life. We recently had a man from New York come to the greenhouses in hopes of finding enough flowering Jasmines to adhere to his family's Buddhist tradition.

Another tradition that we've tried and enjoyed was passed along to us from an Asian gentleman. Pick the flowers from *J. sambac* 'Grand Duke of Tuscany' or 'Maid of Orleans' and place them in a jug of water overnight. The next morning, strain and sip on the now fragrant and pleasing taste of Jasmine

Jasminum parkeri

water. This is a simple and magical way to start your day. Our collections would be incomplete without our beloved Jasmines from around the world.

jasminum

Justicia

The magnificent blooms shower the senses with a cascading fountain of color. Drink from that fountain and remember there is more to its presence than what meets the eye.

BOTANICAL NAME: *Justicia* (jus-tis´-ia)

COMMON NAME: *Shrimp Plant, Brazilian Plume*

FAMILY NAME: *Acanthaceae*

ORIGIN: *South America, Central, Mexico*

Justicia carnea

LIGHT: *full to partial sun*

SIZE AND GROWTH: *1 - 2 feet in container; upright growth habit*

MINIMUM TEMPERATURE: *60°F*

BLOOMING SEASON:
- *J. brandegeana and J. 'Fruit Cocktail': everbloomers*
- *J. rizini: winter*
- *other varieties: spring, summer and fall*

OUTSIDE HARDINESS ZONE: *zone 10 and higher*

SOIL: *any well-drained potting mix*

FERTILIZER: *moderate amounts of fertilizer year-round as long as the temperatures are above 60°F and light levels are high*

BEST TIME TO PRUNE:
- *seasonal bloomers: prune right after flowering cycle*
- *everbloomers: prune whenever growth is too stalky or rangy*

PESTS OR DISEASE TO WATCH FOR:
- *insects: high susceptibility to white fly; some susceptibility to spider mite and minimal to aphids and mealy bug*
- *foliar disease: none except under cool, damp conditions, then problems with Botrytis*
- *root disease: none*

UNIQUE CHARACTERISTICS/OTHER GROWING TIPS:

Justicia are soft growers, which means they grow fast and transpire water freely. When they are put under drought stress, their leaves yellow and their appearance becomes scraggly. Here are three cultural tips for the successful blooming of *Justicias*. First, watch their watering needs closely. Do not let them go into a severe wilt. Second, keep the light levels high. Third, keep steady amounts of fertilizer on these plants as long as the temperatures are above 60°F. To make a full specimen, give *Justicias* a hard pruning. We have had *Justicia* in the same pot for years with the cycle of growth, bloom, and hard pruning year after year. *J. rizini* is one *Justicia* that is more temperamental. It's a winter bloomer and responds to the short day length; it needs one good growing season before it begins to

Above: Justicia brandegeana; above right: Justicia carnea 'Alba'; below right: Justicia 'Fruit Cocktail'

flower. Grow in full sun and don't prune after late spring. In our experience, any deviation from this will create a specimen that doesn't flower.

One of the most famous houseplants is *Justicia brandegeana*, also known as the "Shrimp Plant." Its golden-bronze, shrimp-like sheaves with a protruding white flower have captured the attention of gardeners for decades. Why? The ease of culture, coupled with its reliable year-round bloom, puts the "Shrimp Plant" in a class all by itself.

However, *Justicia carnea*, also known as the "Brazilian Plume," has its own merits. Like feathers on an exotic bird, Brazilian Plume cheerfully bursts forth in a massive show of color. The other four varieties we grow are also unique in style, ease of culture and rapid growth. We continue to use this genus for our display plants because they flower as predictable as the sun rising each day.

Kalanchoe

These brightly colored balloon-like flowers radiate a warmth and endurance that bring solace to the soul.

BOTANICAL NAME: *Kalanchoe* (ka-lan´-ko-ee)
COMMON NAME: *Coral Bells*
FAMILY NAME: *Crassulaceae*
ORIGIN: *Madagascar*

LIGHT: *full to partial sun*
SIZE AND GROWTH:
* *K. manginii, K. pumila: 8 - 10 inches; upright sprawling growth habit*
* *K. uniflora: 1 - 3 inches; trailing growth habit*

MINIMUM TEMPERATURE: *30° - 50°F*
BLOOMING SEASON: *winter*
OUTSIDE HARDINESS ZONE: *zone 10 and higher*
SOIL: *any well-drained potting mix*
FERTILIZER: *moderate amounts of fertilizer throughout active growing season in early fall; restrict feed and reduce during wintertime until flowering is finished and growth resumes*
BEST TIME TO PRUNE: *Important: prune immediately after flowering cycle to insure blooms for the next season*

PESTS OR DISEASE TO WATCH FOR:
* *insects: high susceptibility to mealy bug*
* *foliar disease: none*
* *root disease: let dry out between waterings to prevent root rot*

UNIQUE CHARACTERISTICS/OTHER GROWING TIPS:

These winter bloomers have their rapid growth cycle during the summer. This is the time to increase water and fertilizer to insure robust growth and winter flowers. We recommend keeping nighttime temperatures below 60°F as they go into the fall. They are easily grown houseplants that live happily in a given pot for years. *K. uniflora* is a trailing variety and needs some pruning and encouragement or it will trail to the ground. The other species of *K. pumila* and *K. manginii* will gracefully spill over the containers. We've had them in the same pot for over fifteen years, enjoying their winter show immensely.

Kalanchoes are a major horticultural crop where these upright growing hybrids are used as gift and holiday plants much like Poinsettias. Their popularity stems from the ease of culture and wonderful displays of wintertime blooms. As succulents, *Kalanchoes* are enduring and do well with forgetful watering. When given cool nights and shortening day length, bloom is stimulated and a heavy show of flowers is in store.

Kalanchoes are a large genus with 125 species and numerous hybrids. At Logee's, we grow a few of the more obscure species that have great merit for their compact growth and heavy bloom. We have grown these plants since we've been in business. That's 109 years of winter brightness that we wouldn't have had. It has become a tradition for us to see the familiar sight of *Kalanchoes* cascading from a basket, ringing in the New Year.

Left: Kalanchoe pumila;
below left: Kalanchoe manginii;
below right: Kalanchoe uniflora

kalanchoe

Leonitis

A fiery burst of color heralds in the change of seasons, reminding us that the cycles of life are never-ending.

BOTANICAL NAME: *Leonotis* (lee-o-no´-tis)
COMMON NAME: *Lion's Ear*
FAMILY NAME: *Labiatae*
ORIGIN: *South Africa*

LIGHT: *full sun*
SIZE AND GROWTH: *1¹/₂ - 3 feet in container; upright growth habit*
MINIMUM TEMPERATURE: *40°F*
BLOOMING SEASON: *heavy blooms in fall and early winter; minor flowering sometimes in early spring*
OUTSIDE HARDINESS ZONE: *zone 10 and higher*
SOIL: *any well-drained potting mix*
FERTILIZER: *moderate to high levels of fertilizer during active growing season*
BEST TIME TO PRUNE: *prune hard to severe after flowering, and again during late spring if needed; Lion's Ear will grow out in time for next flowering cycle*
PESTS OR DISEASE TO WATCH FOR:
- *insects: high susceptibility to spider mite; some susceptibility to aphids and white fly*
- *foliar disease: botritis can occur on flowers if stressed with cool conditions*
- *root disease: none*

UNIQUE CHARACTERISTICS/OTHER GROWING TIPS:

Leonotis are spring and fall bloomers with the heaviest show of colors in the fall. One word of caution when growing *Leonotis* — they transpire rapidly and wilt easily. Therefore, attention must be given to drought stress. When grown outside in a container where the roots can reach the soil, be sure to lift the pot several times or the roots will grow outside the pot and take hold. When wintering over, we recommend growing *Leonotis* in a cool sunny spot. If they are given warm conditions with low light levels, they become leggy. The traditional fall mums have their place, but *Leonotis* are an attractive alternative and dress up any October theme.

Leonotis leonorus or "Lion's Ear" is loved for its brilliant orange flowers during the fall months. We recommend starting with three to four young cuttings in June and pot them in a twelve- to fourteen-inch container. Initially, pinch or prune the tips, let them grow out three to four inches, then pinch them again. Within four months, this fast grower will give a great show of color as a two-and-a-half to three-foot plant. A minor species called *L. nepetifolia* is short in height but also grows rapidly. It's a great addition for a mixed container planting, although the flowers are not as brilliant as the flowers of *L. leonorus*.

We also recommend giving *Leonotis* lots of water, for they transpire rapidly and wilt easily. Keep plenty of fertilizer on these heavy feeders and as the day length shortens, buds will appear. Their magnificent show of colors will bring you through the fall months.

Opposite: Leonotis leonorus

leonitis

Mandevilla

A brilliant and cheerful presence that catches the eye and magnetizes the soul.

BOTANICAL NAME: *Mandevilla (man-da-vil´-a)*
COMMON NAME: *Mandevilla*
FAMILY NAME: *Apocynaceae*
ORIGIN: *Central and South America*

LIGHT: *full sun a must*
SIZE AND GROWTH: *1 - 3 feet in container; vining in habit*
MINIMUM TEMPERATURE: *60°F*
BLOOMING SEASON: *spring, summer and fall dependent on the intensity of light*
OUTSIDE HARDINESS ZONE: *zone 10 and higher*
SOIL: *any well-drained potting mix; slightly acidic*
FERTILIZER: *moderate levels of fertilizer during active growth; if light levels are low and temperatures drop below 60°F, stop fertilizer; begin fertilizer again in the spring*
BEST TIME TO PRUNE: *hard prune in late winter to early spring, after their winter dormancy; prune anytime growth is excessive*
PESTS OR DISEASE TO WATCH FOR:
- *insects: high susceptibility to mealy bug; M. laxa (white fragrant variety) has high susceptibility to spider mite; M. x amabilis 'Alice Dupont' has some susceptibility to spider mite*
- *foliar disease: none*
- *root disease: all Mandevillas have problems with root diseases if grown under cool, damp conditions in greenhouses or conservatories, or kept excessively wet*

UNIQUE CHARACTERISTICS/OTHER GROWING TIPS:

M. amabilis and its cultivars are grown in southern nurseries and shipped north for spring outdoor planting. *Mandevillas* must be cultured on the dry side through the winter until active growth begins in February. Root disease is usually not a problem when grown in the home environment where temperatures are high and conditions are dry. We recommend growing *Mandevillas* in clay pots to help keep the root systems healthy. Mature plants are fast growing, and need annual thinning and pruning. If cultured outside in summer, prune back only as necessary when brought inside. The more foliage left on until early spring, the healthier the root system will be.

Mandevillas have showy flowers and make excellent houseplants in a sunny window. They were named for H.J. Mandeville, the British minister of Buenos Aires. *M. sanderi* and *M. amabilis* have good drought resistance and are tolerant to neglectful watering. As long as light levels are high, the lipstick red blossoms of *M. sanderi* 'Red Riding Hood' or the rich pink colors of *M. amabilis* will reward the gardener time and again.

Mandevillas have been especially popular in the last two decades because of the incredible show of flowers for the summer garden. It takes a good size plant to make spectacular shows. Second year plants grown from cuttings will do the trick. They are noted for their ability to climb and vine, and are often used to fill outdoor patio spaces. When given a trellis or support, *Mandevilla* can be grown inside. *M. sanderi* cultivars are compact growers and are perfect for the indoor garden.

Mandevilla amabilis 'Alice Du Pont'

Manettia

Entertaining the beholder, this Twining Firecracker sparks the imagination, bringing pleasure and inspiration during the longest days of the winter.

Manettia luteo rubra

BOTANICAL NAME: *Manettia luteo-rubra (ma-net´-ee-a)*
COMMON NAME: *Twining Firecracker*
FAMILY NAME: *Rubiaceae*
ORIGIN: *Paraguay, Uruguay*

LIGHT: *full to partial sun*
SIZE AND GROWTH: *1 - 2 feet in container; vining in habit*
MINIMUM TEMPERATURE: *60 °F*
BLOOMING SEASON: *spring, fall and winter*
OUTSIDE HARDINESS ZONE: *zone 10 and higher*
SOIL: *any well-drained potting mix*
FERTILIZER: *low to moderate amounts of fertilizer during the growing season; to correct edge burn, it helps to add calcium sulfate (agricultural gypsom) to the fertilizer*
BEST TIME TO PRUNE: *mid-summer when not in bloom or anytime the plant becomes unsightly; if daylight is short, it will quickly come back into bloom*
PESTS OR DISEASE TO WATCH FOR:

• *insects: high susceptibility to white fly*
• *foliar disease: susceptible to leaf spots; flowers can get botrytis if grown under cool damp conditions*
• *root disease: none*

UNIQUE CHARACTERISTICS:

Manettias' vigorous vining habit lends itself to being trained into the "perfect specimen." Beware, even under the best conditions, a tendency exists for the older leaves to die back. We recommend training the new vines to cover the old leaves, which gives the look of a much greener and fuller specimen. Other than their susceptibility to edge burn, they are easy plants to grow and do well in east, west, or south windows.

Just in time for the festivities, *Manettia luteo rubra* or "Twining Firecracker" adds color and style to any holiday gathering. Blooming for six months of the darkest days of the year, this fast grower makes an excellent basket plant. Also attractive in a pot or when trained on a stake or trellis, this *Manettia* is true to its common name.

When *Manettia* is not in flower, it grows rapidly and benefits from regular applications of fertilizer. Once the flowers start to explode, decrease fertilizer, which can help reduce the possibility of browning leaf edges. This common problem, called "edge burn," happens when plants are over fertilized. *Manettias* are susceptible to edge burn. We believe that is why this cheery plant has never made it to the wholesale horticultural trade. Yet, with close attention to fertilizer and growing conditions, this is a wonderful pant, especially during the wintertime.

Michelia

When the sun shines upon these fragile flowers, a delightful fragrance is activated; when darkness falls, the sweet scent becomes only a memory.

BOTANICAL NAME: *Michelia figo* (meu-chell-ee´-a)
COMMON NAME: *Banana Shrub*
FAMILY NAME: *Magnoliaceae*
ORIGIN: *China*

LIGHT: *full or partial sun*
SIZE AND GROWTH: *1 - 3 feet in container; upright growth habit*
MINIMUM TEMPERATURE: *35 °F*
BLOOMING SEASON: *year-round, heaviest in spring*
OUTSIDE HARDINESS ZONE: *zone 8 and higher*
SOIL: *any well-drained potting mix*
FERTILIZER: *moderate amounts of fertilizer year-round, although do not over fertilize in winter; susceptible to iron chlorosis — add chelated iron to fertilizer*
BEST TIME TO PRUNE: *in summer after the heaviest show of flowers in the spring, or prune anytime growth is excessive*
PESTS OR DISEASE TO WATCH FOR:
- *insects: high susceptibility to mealy bug*
- *foliar disease: some susceptibility in propagation*
- *root disease: some susceptibility if kept wet in the wintertime*

UNIQUE CHARACTERISTICS/OTHER GROWING TIPS:
The most unique aspect of this slow growing "Banana Shrub" is its delightful fragrance that is activated as the sun shines on it. We recommend a southeast or west window on a windowsill, or in a conservatory. Grow tight in a pot. Its shiny leaves help it withstand dry conditions. Be warned though — the flowers are fragile and will fall apart if touched. Flowers form the freest on the axillary buds of woody shoots and not as easily on young, soft growth.

Michelia figo has a pleasant, sweet, banana scent, hence its common name, "Banana Shrub." Flowering year-round, this slow grower needs one to two years from a young cutting before it blooms well. However, this speed of growth lends well to a long-term potted plant, as *Michelio* doesn't mind being grown tight in a pot.

Michelia figo

Flowers last only a day and are fragile. They only exude their fragrance when the sun shines on them. On a sunny day in Canton, China, the entire city smells like sweet bananas from the pervasive Banana Shrub planted throughout the city. Although *Michelia* has periods of heavy bloom, it sporadically flowers throughout the year except in the dead of winter.

michelia

Mitriostigma

Giving intoxicating pleasure, an overwhelming intensity of sweetness emerges from these pink-tinged blossoms in an endless flow of fragrance.

BOTANICAL NAME: *Mitriostigma axillare (mi-tree-o´-stig-ma)*
COMMON NAME: *African Gardenia*
FAMILY NAME: *Rubiaceae*
ORIGIN: *South Africa*

LIGHT: *full to partial sun*
SIZE AND GROWTH: *1¹/₂ - 2 feet in container; upright in habit*
MINIMUM TEMPERATURE: *55°F*
BLOOMING SEASON: *everbloomer*
OUTSIDE HARDINESS ZONE: *zone 10 and higher*
SOIL: *any well-drained potting mix*
FERTILIZER: *moderate amounts of fertilizer year-round*
BEST TIME TO PRUNE: *anytime; does well with severe pruning; sprouts out easily*
PESTS OR DISEASE TO WATCH FOR:
 • *insects: high susceptibility to scale and mealy bug*
 • *foliar disease: none*
 • *root disease: some susceptibility*

UNIQUE CHARACTERISTICS/OTHER GROWING TIPS:

Did you know the size and shape of a young *Mitriostigma* depends on where the cutting was taken? If an upright shoot was taken, then it will grow more upright. If a lateral shoot was taken, then it will be low growing and sprawling. However, in time, upright growth will dominate and pruning will eventually determine the final shape of the plant. To get a bushy, full specimen, prune often. Flower buds form in clusters at the leaf axis and emerge over long periods of time. Blooms re-flower from leaf nodes time and again. *Mitriostigma* is a close relative of the coffee plant and has a similar growth habit.

Many of the growing difficulties arise from root disease. Common complaints are stunted growth and lack of leaf luster and vigor. To remedy these problems, grow in bright light, clay containers and don't over pot. Be sure the soil dries out between waterings, with a slight wilt on a regular basis. They are not fast growers but once mature, flowers can always be found and enjoyed. In tropical and sub-tropical areas, *Mitriostigma* is reported as not doing well. We believe this is still a result of an unhealthy root system. Follow the above recommendations and reap the benefits of a fragrant house-plant year-round.

Although its common name is African Gardenia, this plant is not a gardenia at all, only a distant relative. What it does have in common with the Gardenias is fragrance. *Mitriostigma axillare* flowers year-round and is much easier to grow than Gardenias. And as far as fragrance goes, the blooms are sweet and mild. Its attractive, shiny, lance-like leaves and bushy habit make this African Gardenia a treat to grow.

We originally acquired *Mitriostigma axillare* through the Brooklyn Botanic Gardens. They had contracted four or five nurseries in the New York and New Jersey areas to grow 20,000 plants for them. The Botanic Gardens thought this new introduction would make a lovely membership gift. After considerable effort, the nurseries could not mass-produce *Mitriostigma* in time for the gift giving. Finally, one of the nurseries gave up and released their stock plant to us in1973. We have had it ever since. We haven't had any trouble with *Mitriostigma*. It only needs attention to watering and a little patience.

Mitriostigma axillare

Mucuna

Fiery orange flowers emerge in brilliance as they climb and display their full potential.

BOTANICAL NAME: *Mucuna species*
COMMON NAME: *Mucuna*
FAMILY NAME: *Leguminosae*
ORIGIN: *Brazilian*

LIGHT: *full to partial sun*
SIZE AND GROWTH: *minimum 3 - 4 feet; heavy vine*
MINIMUM TEMPERATURE: *55 °F*
BLOOMING SEASON: *winter*
OUTSIDE HARDINESS ZONE: *zone 10 and higher*
SOIL: *any well-drained potting mix*
FERTILIZER: *moderate amounts of fertilizer throughout the year*
BEST TIME TO PRUNE: *important to prune immediately after flowering to insure next years blooms; prune severely — cut back to woody growth once a year, then do not prune again until after next flowering cycle*
PESTS OR DISEASE TO WATCH FOR:
- *insects: high susceptibility to spider mite*
- *foliar disease: none*
- *root disease: none*

UNIQUE CHARACTERISTICS:

Mucuna species is a heavy vine that needs space for growth. As a potted plant, it needs to be grown in a large container and given a strong support. Supports such as trellis or stakes work well for its vigorous growth. Young plants need to obtain some size before flowering. In our experience, for *Mucuna species* to come into bloom, the plant has to be heavily foliated on at least a three-foot support in a ten-inch pot. Then, it will bud up nicely. Once plants are finished blooming they can be pruned.

We prune in late January or February, then do not prune again until after the next flowering season. Throughout the summer months, we recommend that you wrap the vine around itself. One of the more famous *Mucunas*, *bennetii*, known as the "Guinea Creeper," is a spectacular tropical climber with immense flowers. We have tried culturing it in pots but have found that it grows much better when planted directly into the ground.

Nothing short of spectacular, this large, heavy climber shows off its orange opposing flowers that dangle on its long pendulous chain. Unlike other varieties, this *Mucuna* will flower in a container. We grow them in twelve- to sixteen-inch pots, which support their vigorous growth adequately.

Two seasons of growth are needed before it will flower freely. But it is well worth the wait, as these fiery orange flowers arrive in the dead of winter. It propagates easily. We use mature leaves on a young stem cutting. The mature leaves on older stem do not work as well. We like to give *Mucuna species* lots of room to vine around the greenhouses, where its racemes of flowers can pendulate amongst its vigorous growing vine. We often recommend *Mucuna species* as a conservatory plant or in a sunroom where space for growth is available.

the plants

Mucuna species

Murraya

A sweet fragrance permeates the senses reminding us that the full expression of life's passion is an internal experience.

BOTANICAL NAME: *Murraya* (mur-ra´-ya)
COMMON NAME: *Orange Jasmine, Lake View Jasmine, Mock Orange, Curry Leaf*
FAMILY NAME: *Rutaceae*
ORIGIN: *China, South India, Australia*

LIGHT: *full sun to partial sun*
SIZE AND GROWTH: *1 - 2 feet in container; upright growth habit*
MINIMUM TEMPERATURE: *45°F*
BLOOMING SEASON: *everbloomer, heaviest in summer*
OUTSIDE HARDINESS ZONE: *zone 10 and higher*
SOIL: *any well-drained potting mix; slightly acidic*
FERTILIZER: *low to moderate levels of fertilizer from spring to fall; susceptible to iron chlorosis so add chelated iron*
BEST TIME TO PRUNE: *anytime after heaviest bloom of summer; prune from fall to winter*
PESTS OR DISEASE TO WATCH FOR:
- *insects: no susceptibility*
- *foliar disease: none*
- *root disease: some susceptibility to root rot in winter under cool temperatures*

UNIQUE CHARACTERISTICS/OTHER GROWING TIPS:

Murrayas are fragrant, rugged growers and make good indoor plants. They are tolerant to a wide variety of light levels and emit a sweet, heavy, orange scent. Two *Murrayas* that have similar leaf and flower structure are *M. paniculata* and *M. exotica*. *M. paniculata*, which came to us from the University of Connecticut botany department, is a compact growing shrub. Its leaves and branches are held tightly in form. As a mature plant, the upright growth habit is heavily branched. *M. exotica* has a more sprawling habit, with larger leaves and flowers. It's a strong grower but takes longer to come into bloom and does not flower as heavily.

The third *Murrayas* we grow is *M. koenigii* or the "Curry Leaf." Its pungent leaves are used as an ingredient in a curry spice mix. The flowers are not fragrant. Related to many container plants, *Murrayas* are slow growing, which make them good candidates for windowsill culture. They are easily maintained in size. The greatest flowering occurs from early spring through fall with waves of heavy bloom throughout. *Murraya paniculata* is the freest-flowering variety and after pruning, quickly re-sprouts. However, since it is a slow grower, we recommend selectively pruning the leads.

One of the finest *Murrayas* for pot culture is *M. paniculata*. It has a tight growth habit and intense orange-scented blooms, with the heaviest flowering occurring in summertime. *Murrayas* in general are rugged growers and tolerant to a wide range of light levels.

M. paniculata and "Lakeview Jasmine", or *M. exotica*, have often been confused for the same plant. However, Lakeview Jasmine has a more sprawling growth habit and does not bloom as heavily. It

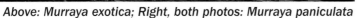
Above: Murraya exotica; Right, both photos: Murraya paniculata

branches and reaches outward, almost growing sideways. In the warm areas of the south, Lakeview Jasmine is grown as a hedge, as shearing creates thick dense foliage. The leaves are large and more pointed. Another *Murraya*, called *M. koengii*, is not grown for its flowers but for its culinary foliage.

Neomarica

This Walking Iris expresses timeless beauty in the moment.

BOTANICAL NAME: *Neomarica gracilis (nee-o-ma-ree´-ca)*
COMMON NAME: *Walking Iris*
FAMILY NAME: *Iradaceae*
ORIGIN: *Tropical Americas, South Mexico, Northern Brazil*

LIGHT: *partial sun to shade; will tolerate higher light levels*
SIZE AND GROWTH: *2 feet in container*
MINIMUM TEMPERATURE: *50 °F*
BLOOMING SEASON: *mid-winter*
OUTSIDE HARDINESS ZONE: *zone 10 and higher*
SOIL: *any well-drained potting mix*
FERTILIZER: *low amounts of fertilizer during active growing season; not heavy feeders*
BEST TIME TO PRUNE: *prune off plantlets; prune older plants immediately after flowering*
PESTS OR DISEASE TO WATCH FOR:
- *insects: none*
- *foliar disease: none*
- *root disease: none*

UNIQUE CHARACTERISTICS/OTHER GROWING TIPS:
Flowering stems of *Neomarica gracilis* emerge out of fan-like leaves. Plantlets then grow from where the flowers have emerged. These young plants, if left to their own, will develop into large plants. For display purposes, remove the plantlets and allow the growth to come from the original plant. Offshoots will sprout from the base of the original plant, which in time create a full specimen. In the coming growing season, new flower stems will be created. If the plantlets are not removed, then as they grow, the weight of the plantlets bend the stem to the ground. If given the chance, they will root into the ground forming a new plant. Hence, its common name, "Walking Iris."

We grow *Neomarica* in full sun to shade; flowers form easily, regardless of light level. The growth habit involves an upright stem from which leaves emerge in a fan-like fashion as a plant matures. After many years, the plant will get so full of growth that it will become unstable. Repotting is an option. We grow them up to a ten-inch pot and then divide. This is done by cutting the root ball in half or into quarters and then repotting them. If some of the stems have grown too tall and become unsightly, they can be cut back to one-inch from the soil. This allows the plant to re-sprout lower down and helps thin out excessive growth.

The Walking Iris is loved for its ease of culture and fragrant colorful blooms. Flowers only last one day but continue to re-emerge out of the stem. The pure white flower with a chocolate, mottled center resembles the shape of an iris and blooms in waves during the winter months. It makes a wonderful houseplant and can be contained in the same pot for many years with little pruning. We are always delighted to go into the greenhouses on a winter day and find one of our large specimens covered with flowers. Taking a moment to breathe in their fragrance, we are literally transported to the tropics and completely forget about the cold conditions outside.

Neomarica gracilis

neomarica

Pachystachys

The Lollipop Flower brings joy and happiness year-round as its brilliance reaches upward.

Pachystachys coccinea

BOTANICAL NAME: *Pachystachys (pa-kee-sta´-kis)*
COMMON NAME:
P. lutea: Lollipop Flower;
P. coccinea: Cardinal's Guard
FAMILY NAME: *Acanthaceae*
ORIGIN: *Peru*

LIGHT: *full to partial sun; better with diffusion or partial sun*
SIZE AND GROWTH: *1 - 3 feet in container; upright growth habit*
MINIMUM TEMPERATURE: *60°F*
BLOOMING SEASON: *everbloomer*
OUTSIDE HARDINESS ZONE: *zone 10 and higher*
SOIL: *any well-drained potting mix*
FERTILIZER: *moderate to heavy amounts of fertilizer, especially during growing season*
BEST TIME TO PRUNE:
- *P. lutea: anytime*
- *P. coccinea: immediately after flowering cycle*

PESTS OR DISEASE TO WATCH FOR:
- *insects: high susceptibility to white fly; minor susceptibility to spider mites and aphids*
- *foliar disease: none*
- *root disease: none*

UNIQUE CHARACTERISTICS/OTHER GROWING TIPS:
The Lollipop Flower is a reliable bloomer and fast grower. It responds well to severe pruning. Remove all the foliage from the plant and it will re-sprout quickly.

Its ability to grow under lower light or full sun makes this a desirable cultivar for the home environment. If it's not in flower, check the light levels. Although preferring some shade, if light levels are too low, it will go out of bloom. *Pachystachys* can be maintained in eight- to ten-inch pots by adding fertilizer and regular pruning.

You can grow mature specimens for eight to ten months before they get too scraggly or loose. Then we recommend a severe pruning. This cycle of growing out, blooming, and then severely pruning can be followed year after year. One note of caution: during the summer, if *Pachystachys* is grown under high light, the foliage may become brassy looking. The plant is not harmed; however, it does not look as lush as those grown under some light diffusion.

Pachystachys are reliable bloomers and easy to grow. *P. lutea* is a yellow variety that flowers in upward spires, and literally looks like lollipops. The yellow bracts (not the flowers) catch the eye. The white blooms emerge from the sides and add to its splendor.

At the greenhouses, we use *Pachystachys* for our display plants because they are always in bloom. They grow better under moderate light levels rather than full sun. Therefore, *Pachystachys* do well in homes with an eastern, southeastern or western exposure. *P. coccinea* is a variety less often grown and has exaggerated internodes, which gives it height. Flowering mostly in the summertime, this Peruvian native displays dazzling bright red colors.

pachystachys

Passiflora

The intricacy of color and form inspires passion in those who seek love and beauty.

BOTANICAL NAME: *Passiflora* (pa-si-flo´-ra)
COMMON NAME: *Passionflower*
FAMILY NAME: *Passifloraceae*
ORIGIN: *Throughout the Americas*

LIGHT: *full sun*
SIZE AND GROWTH: *1 - 3 feet in container; vining growth habit*
MINIMUM TEMPERATURE: *see chart*
BLOOMING SEASON: *see chart*
OUTSIDE HARDINESS ZONE: *zone 7, 8, 9, 10 and higher depending on the variety*
SOIL: *any well-drained potting mix; keep soil pH moderately acidic between 5.8 - 6.2*
FERTILIZER: *low to moderate amounts of fertilizer year-round as long as temperatures are above 60°F; over fertilization is a major problem; plants do best in poor soil*
BEST TIME TO PRUNE: *for most, prune after flowering; for the everbloomers, prune anytime growth is excessive; most respond well to severe pruning*

PESTS OR DISEASE TO WATCH FOR:
• *insects: high susceptibility to spider mite; some susceptibility to mealy bug*
• *foliar disease: in some varieties*
• *root disease: susceptible in some varieties if excessive moisture and cool temperatures*

UNIQUE CHARACTERISTICS/ OTHER GROWING TIPS:

Passionflowers are fast, vigorous growers. Their flowers only last a day but come out in prolific numbers during the blooming cycle. On older vines, when the leaves get yellow and the plant gets scruffy looking, prune hard to rejuvenate the plant. The strength of the root system and its ability to resist root diseases varies from cultivar to cultivar. *P. incarnata* and its hybrids tend to show weakness during the winter. Therefore, we frequently graft these varieties on to *P. x alato-caerulea* to give them a strong root system. In general, we recommend growing passionflowers tight in a pot or planting them outside in poor soil. If they are grown under high fertility, they do not flower well. Giving a balanced fertilizer and high light levels will help insure flowering. In their native habitat, they tend to grow in areas of low fertility. Some of the hybrids and species such as *P. coccinea*, *P. vitifolia* and *P. incarnata* are the exceptions to this rule and flower well, regardless of fertility levels.

However, if your passionflower fails to bloom in its season, the next area to check is light level. They must have full sun to flower well. A great way to maintain passionflowers in containers is to grow them in hanging baskets, wrapping the vines around themselves. When in flower, they create beautiful displays.

Passionflowers have long been admired for their magnificent blooms and their ancient history. According to Brazilian lore, the Spanish missionaries saw these beautiful climbing flowers and interpreted their presence as a sign from God that the native people should be converted to

Top: *Passiflora* 'Elizabeth';
above: *Passiflora* 'Coral Glow'

NAME	COLOR	MIN. TEMP	BLOOMING SEASON
P. 'Coral Glow'	red, burgundy	45°F	spring, fall
P. coccinea	red	60°F	winter
P. coriacea COMMON NAME: *Bat-Leaf Passion Flower*	(grown for foliage)	60°F	everbloomer
P. edulis	white	50°F	spring, summer
P. 'Elizabeth'	dusky lavender	40°F	spring, summer, fall
P. incarnata COMMON NAME: *Maypop*	lavender	40°F	summer
P. incense	royal purple	40°F	summer
P. 'Jeannette'	deep purple	50°F	everbloomer
P. nephrodes	pink, lavender	50°F	spring, summer, fall
P. palmeri	pink fuchsia	45°F	everbloomer
P. pura-vida	dark blue	45°F	everbloomer
P. quadrangulares COMMON NAME: *Lowlands*	purple, white	45°F	spring, summer, fall
P. saint rule	white	50°F	spring, summer
P. sanguinolenta	pink	40°F	spring, summer
P. 'Sapphire'	white, purple	45°F	spring, summer, fall
P. 'Star of Bristol'	lavender, white	40°F	everbloomer
P. 'Star of Clevedon'	white, lavender	45°F	everbloomer
P. violacea Form #3	reddish, purple	45°F	everbloomer
P. vitifolia COMMON NAME: *Crimson Passion Flower*	red	60°F	everbloomer
P. x alato-caerulea	purple, white	45°F	everbloomer
P. x decaisneana	red, purple, white	45°F	summer, fall
P. x kewensis	pink	40°F	spring, summer, fall

passiflora

Pictured, clockwise from lower left: P. 'Star of Clevedon, P. Blue Bouquet, P. 'Byron Beauty', P. coccinea. Right-hand page, clockwise from lower left: P. violacea form #3, P. alata 'Ruby Glow', P. citrina.

Christianity. They told the native Brazilians that the petals represented the Disciples of Christ. The filaments represented the crown of thorns, also known as the corona. The sepals represented the five wounds, and the stamen represented the three nails. The three-pointed, classic passionflower leaf represented the holy trinity.

Passionflowers, long before the missionaries, have always been revered for their mystical qualities. Their intricate coloring and incredible flower form intrigues the senses. And their ability to vine, climb and prolifically bloom also captures the attention of any passerby.

In the greenhouses, this family has become a passion of ours too. We grow over two dozen varieties. Some are unique for their fragrance, while others impress us with their multi-colored patterns. Some produce the ever-desirable passion fruit, while others simply bloom year-round. We are always on a constant vigil, in search of the perfect passionflower.

Each variety has a perfection of its own. Their vines need support and they are excellent candidates for training on wire hoops. Also, try them on trellis or stakes. The vining growth can be wrapped around itself to form a full, bushy specimen.

the plants

passiflora

111

Pavonia

Always rising up and reaching higher, these purple flowers seem to connect Heaven and Earth.

Pavonia multiflora

BOTANICAL NAME: *Pavonia multiflora (pa-vown´-ee-a)*
COMMON NAME: *Many Flowers*
FAMILY NAME: *Malvaceae*
ORIGIN: *Brazil*

LIGHT: *full to partial sun*
SIZE AND GROWTH: *2-4 feet in container; upright growth habit*
MINIMUM TEMPERATURE: *55 °F*
BLOOMING SEASON: *everbloomer*
OUTSIDE HARDINESS ZONE: *zone 10 and higher*
SOIL: *any well-drained potting mix*

FERTILIZER: *moderate levels of fertilizer year-round*
BEST TIME TO PRUNE: *anytime growth is excessive; responds well to severe pruning down to leafless stems which easily re-sprout; will take two months to come back into bloom*
PESTS OR DISEASE TO WATCH FOR:
• *insects: some susceptibility to white fly and spider mite; minor susceptibility to aphids*
• *foliar disease: none*
• *root disease: none*

UNIQUE CHARACTERISTICS/ OTHER GROWING TIPS:

Pavonia multiflora grows better with nighttime temperatures above 60°F. They are easy to grow and do well in an east, west or south window. They will not flower in full shade. Much like a tulip, the flower bract never opens. Older plants can be kept for years by following the simple cycle of growth, flowering, and pruning. Since they are upright growers, they need height in the growing area to accommodate their tall slender stems. The biggest challenge is to create a multiple-stemmed plant, which creates a full, spectacular color. A red calyx with purple protruding stamens makes *Pavonia multiflora* an unusual addition to any home.

True to its name, "many flowers" appear on this *Pavonia* year-round. We can count on blooms for eight to ten months of the year. Even under partial sun conditions, *P. multiflora* never disappoints us. These bright red bracts even appear in the dead of winter.

To get a full specimen, we recommend several prunings when the plant is young. Cut back the stems three to four inches from the soil. Then allow four inches of growth and pinch back again. This will thicken the growth and create multiple stems. Flower buds form up the stem and bloom in vertical succession.

Plants can grow up to six feet with the top foot only producing flowers. After eight months of growing, and looking up at flowers instead of down, prune back the excessive height.

the plants

Pelargonium

With scented foliage, the magic of Pelargoniums is seen in their ability to transport one to a different time and space.

BOTANICAL NAME: *Pelargonium (pe-lar-gon´-nee-um)*
COMMON NAME: *Scented Geranium*
FAMILY NAME: *Geraniaceae*
ORIGIN: *Africa*

LIGHT: *full sun*
SIZE AND GROWTH: *10 - 24 inches in container; upright growth habit*
MINIMUM TEMPERATURE: *35°F*
BLOOMING SEASON: *spring, early summer; need cool nights in winter*
OUTSIDE HARDINESS ZONE: *zone 10 and higher*
SOIL: *any well-drained potting mix*
FERTILIZER: *low to moderate amounts of fertilizer; if over fertilized, it will get leggy and have soft growth*
BEST TIME TO PRUNE: *after flowering in the summertime, or in late fall or early winter*
PESTS OR DISEASE TO WATCH FOR:
- *insects: occasional susceptibility to aphids and white fly*
- *foliar disease: high susceptibility to botrytis if under damp conditions*
- *root disease: some susceptibility to root rot*

UNIQUE CHARACTERISTICS/ OTHER GROWING TIPS:

To induce flowering, give Geraniums cool nighttime temperatures below 60°F. We recommend keeping the temperatures between 35°F and 55°F under high sunlight during the wintertime as the day length starts to increase. Keep them in full sun and grow on the dry side in clay pots. They do better when grown under lower fertilization, high light, and give a little drought stress from time to time. We bring our stock plants outside in the springtime and plant them directly into the ground. Their favorite spot is near the greenhouse where there is only sand, no loam or fertilizer. This environment turns them into beautiful compact specimens with tight internodes. If they are planted in fertile ground, the plants look leggy and have soft growth. Don't be mistaken — they make a great houseplant for a sunny

Pelargonium 'Dean's Delight'

window. Just remember to keep them cool and on the dry side.

If they become thin and scraggly, like all Geraniums, they respond well to a hard pruning. They will sprout right out, and in no time, full lush specimens will return. **PLEASE NOTE:** it is cool

pelargonium

Above: Pelargonium 'Apricot'; right: P. 'Red-Flowered Rose'

weather that initiates flowering and keeps them flowering; therefore, when spring goes into summer and temperatures become warmer, they stop flowering.

Scented Geraniums hold a revered place in the heart of Logee's. Joy Logee Martin, who is now 90 years old, has collected scented Geraniums for the past seventy years. It was this love for the scented Geranium that brought Logee's into the mail-order business. In the 1930s, Joy wanted to find others who loved her Geraniums as much as she did. She made a list and sent it to her horticultural friends. From that day on, Logee's became a major leader in the catalog/shipping industry of tropical container plants.

At Logees, we grow fifty-three scented Geraniums, which are known for their fragrant foliage. We have fruit, rose, lemon, oak, and pine-scented Geraniums. They make wonderful container plants and, although we've been growing them since the twenties, only within the last two decades have they become mainstream plants.

Our children love to walk into the scented-Geranium greenhouse, rub the foliage and guess the different smells. Besides the fragrance, many of these Geraniums have outstanding flowers as well.

The rose-scented Geraniums have many good bloomers such as P. 'Sweet Mariam', P. 'Tiny Gem' and P. 'Red Flowered Rose'. The lemon-scented Geraniums boast P. 'Lemon Crispum' and P. 'Prince Rupert'. Both have a pleasing, crisp lemon fragrance. Plus, P. 'Prince Rupert' has attractive variegated foliage. The mint-scented rose geranium is pleasing in beauty and diversity. The fruit-scented strawberry is one of our favorites for its fragrance and flowers.

the plants

The translucent, brilliant yellow center illuminates all aspects of beauty, inside and out.

BOTANICAL NAME: *Pereskia grandifolia (per-ees-key´-a)*
COMMON NAME: *Rose Cactus*
FAMILY NAME: *Cactaceae*
ORIGIN: *New World, Central and South America, Brazil*

LIGHT: *full sun*
SIZE AND GROWTH: *1 - 3 feet in container; upright growth habit*
MINIMUM TEMPERATURE: *50°F*
BLOOMING SEASON: *spring, summer, fall*
OUTSIDE HARDINESS ZONE: *zone 10 and higher*
SOIL: *cactus soil or any well-drained potting mix*
FERTILIZER: *give low amounts of fertilizer at regular intervals; do not fertilize in the winter when they are resting*
BEST TIME TO PRUNE: *hard pruning in late winter or early spring will still allow flowers for the coming season*
PESTS OR DISEASE TO WATCH FOR:
• *insects: occasional susceptibility to mealy bug and aphids*
• *foliar disease: none*
• *root disease: none*

UNIQUE CHARACTERISTICS/OTHER GROWING TIPS:

Pereskia grandifolia needs to dry out between waterings. It is normal for leaf drop to occur during the dormancy period of winter. Do not be alarmed if *Pereskia* completely defoliates. This is normal. Generally we propagate by vegetative cutting during active growth. It is best to have mature leaves and stems to propagate. CAUTION: When handling, be careful of thorns that come out of the stem.

Pereskia grandifolia is an excellent patio container plant and also makes a wonderful addition to any sunny room. The flowers continue to emerge in clusters from new shoots creating a continuous show of bloom. From the cactus family, *Pereskia grandifolia* is tolerant to dryness and will tolerate some neglectful watering, especially during winter. Yet, it is a fast grower during the summer months, and attention to watering will help achieve good growth and flowering. In the winter months, we recommend decreasing the water. As a general rule, grow this Rose Cactus in clay pots to allow a drying out between waterings.

Pereskia grandifolia

Phalenopsis Orchid

Exotic-looking, the cascading floral display invites a fullness of expression into any living space.

BOTANICAL NAME: *Phalaenopsis (fell-lie-nop´-sis)*
COMMON NAME: *Moth Orchid*
FAMILY NAME: *Orchidaceae*
ORIGIN: *Southeast Asia, Philippines*

LIGHT: *partial sun to shade*
SIZE AND GROWTH: *12 inches in container; upright growth habit*
MINIMUM TEMPERATURE: *60°F*
BLOOMING SEASON: *fall, winter, spring; mature plants flower nearly year-round*
OUTSIDE HARDINESS ZONE: *zone 10 and higher*
SOIL: *grow in epiphytic orchid mix, ie: fir bark, long fiber sphagnum moss, or commercial orchid mix*
FERTILIZER: *fertilization depends upon which media they're grown in — bark mix needs highest levels of fertilizer; sphagnum moss doesn't need as much fertilizer because it retains fertilizer easier*
BEST TIME TO PRUNE: *doesn't need pruning; just needs grooming*
PESTS OR DISEASE TO WATCH FOR:
• *insects: resistant to insects; low susceptibility to scale (only if near infected plants); low susceptibility to broad mite*
• *foliar disease: high susceptibility to bacteria leaf spots*
• *root disease: susceptibility to root rot*

UNIQUE CHARACTERISTICS/OTHER GROWING TIPS:

In a home situation, we do not recommend forcing the plants with high levels of fertilizer because the roots are sensitive to high salt levels. Their epiphytic nature only requires low to moderate levels of fertilizer. There are two difficulties when growing orchids: first, maintaining a healthy root system; second, getting the orchid to come into flower.

To maintain a healthy root system, plants grown in a commercial mix or bark mix need to be repotted every 12 to 18 months. Why? Because the media starts to break down making the roots decay. We grow our Phalaenopsis in long fiber sphagnum moss. The roots stay healthier in this mix and we don't have to repot as often.

Another tip to maintain a healthy root system is to pay close attention to watering. How should you water? Bark mixes or commercial mixes often have fir bark in them. The surface of the exposed media dries quickly, making it difficult to tell when the roots of the orchid are dry. Therefore, we recommend a watering schedule, such as once a week. If you're potting orchids in sphagnum moss, then we recommend watering them according to the moisture level of the medium, which is visible at the top of the pot. When the media has changed from dark to light (or wet to dry), then wait one day and thoroughly water the plant the next. We recommend growing orchids in clay pots for a quicker dry down.

The most common question we get about *Phalaenopsis* is 'why won't it flower?' The young plants need a period in the fall where temperatures drop into the mid-fifties at night for at least one month. They also need increased light levels to stimulate the flower

the plants

Phalenopsis hybrid

bud or spike formation. Once you have a mature orchid, then it will flower, regardless of cool nighttime temperatures.

Another common question is, 'Why are my leaves shriveling?' This is a common problem with *Phalaenopsis*. The older leaves start to shrivel because they are not getting enough water or their root system has collapsed. Check the roots: there may not be any roots to take up the water.

The last concern is foliar disease. Do not leave moisture on the leaves. High moisture levels with high humidity and stagnant air are the breeding ground for bacterial diseases.

Much to contrary belief, some of the easiest plants to grow in the home are *Phalaenopsis* orchids. They are very adaptable to the home environment and have a long flowering cycle. A single *Phalaenopsis* flower can last as long as one month, with the flowering cycle lasting between eight to ten weeks or longer.

In their native land, *Phalaenopsis* are found in the mid-stories of the jungle canopy. Growing on the sides of trees, the light levels are somewhat low. Since they are epiphytes, they go through intermittent periods of dryness with plenty of air around their roots. A home has many environmental conditions similar to their native habitat, not only in dryness but also the moderate light levels and warm temperatures. *Phalaenopsis* are resilient plants too. Unlike many tropical plants, if a cultural problem arises, there is more time to correct it. As one orchid grower says, "Orchids die slowly."

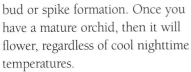

Phaseolus

Fast growth and unique lavendar flowers make this vine stand out.

Phaseolus carcalla

BOTANICAL NAME: *Phaseolus carcalla (fa-see´-o-lus)*
COMMON NAME: *Snail Flower*
FAMILY NAME: *Legumaceae*
ORIGIN: *Tropical Americas*

LIGHT: *full sun*
SIZE AND GROWTH: *2 - 3 feet; vining in habit*
MINIMUM TEMPERATURE: *55°F*
BLOOMING SEASON: *spring, summer, fall*
OUTSIDE HARDINESS ZONE: *zone 10 and higher*
SOIL: *any well-drained potting mix*
FERTILIZER: *low to moderate levels of fertilizer year-round except winter*
BEST TIME TO PRUNE: *anytime*
PESTS OR DISEASE TO WATCH FOR:
• *insects: high susceptibility to spider mite*
• *foliar disease: none*
• *root disease: none*
UNIQUE CHARACTERISTICS/OTHER GROWING TIPS:

This three-season bloomer grows fast and is easy to culture. Growing as fast as its relative the pole bean, *Phaseolus* needs pruning weekly. Botanically, there is a great deal of confusion with the two names, *Phaseolus* and *Vigna* being interchanged. Plants sold on the West Coast as *Vigna* are often what we call *Phaseolus*. When used as a summer climber, it is important not to over fertilize. Too much fertilizer will only give it vegetative, not floral growth. We have a vine that has been planted in the ground at the greenhouses for over fifty years. It never gets fertilized and blooms ten months of the year.

Phaseolus is related to the common pole bean. And much like its relative, *Phaseolus* is an exceptionally fast grower. Its giant lavender flower, coiled and shaped like a snail, attracts all that pass by. Another fascinating feature of this *Phaseolus* is its pollination mechanism. As the bee lands on the flower, the stamen and pistils emerge from the coil. Then, when the bee flies away, the stamen and pistils go back into the coil and pollinate the flower. This vine grows so fast in the greenhouses that we have to prune it on a weekly basis year-round.

If you're looking for a good summertime plant to fill in a patio or climb up a trellised wall, we recommend Snail Flower. Not only is it attractive, but its cultural requirements are low. Plant in poor soil and give minimum, if any, fertilizer and the flowers will come in abundance. The Snail Flower also works well in a sunny window, especially if you want vegetative growth fast.

Plectranthus

Spires of pink rise up to bring a breath of softness to the eyes and senses.

BOTANICAL NAME: *Plectranthus* (plek-tranth´-us)
COMMON NAME: *Plectranthus*
FAMILY NAME: *Labiatae*
ORIGIN: *South Africa*

LIGHT:
- *P. fruiticosa: full to partial sun*
- *P. hilliardiae: full to partial shade*

SIZE AND GROWTH:
- *P. fruiticosa: 18 - 24 inches*
- *P. hilliardiae 8 - 10 inches; upright growth habit*

MINIMUM TEMPERATURE: *50°F*

BLOOMING SEASON:
- *P. fruiticosa: fall*
- *P. hilliardiae: fall through winter*

OUTSIDE HARDINESS ZONE: *zone 10 and higher*

SOIL: *any well-drained potting mix*

FERTILIZER: *low to moderate levels of fertilizer during active growing season from spring to fall; reduce or eliminate in the wintertime*

BEST TIME TO PRUNE: *after flowering*

PESTS OR DISEASE TO WATCH FOR:
- *insects: P. hilliardiae occasional susceptibility to mealy bug; P. fruiticosa has high susceptibility to white fly and some susceptibility to spider mite and mealy bug*
- *foliar disease: none*
- *root disease: none*

UNIQUE CHARACTERISTICS /OTHER GROWING TIPS:

These two *Plectranthus* give us their most abundant show of flowers in the fall. They are daylight sensitive, responding to the shortened day length. *P. hilliardiae* intermittently blooms throughout the year with its heaviest flowering in late summer and fall. *P. fruiticosa* is a rapid and easy grower. In June, we start with young plants and pinch them back. If you start with a mature plant, then cut it back hard by June 1. Then do not cut back again. Place in full sun for summer growth. By late summer, buds will start to form and by mid-fall, it will come into full bloom. After flowering, cut back and win-

Plectranthus hilliadiae

ter over. In late spring, do one more pruning and start the cycle all over again. *P. hilliardiae* is similar except it's lower growing and will take much lower light levels. This plant grew in our office in a north window for a year and never went out of bloom. We grow six varieties

plectranthus

Plectranthus fruiticosa

of *Plectranthus*. *P. hilliardiae* and *P. fruiticosa* have the showiest blooms. The other *Plectranthus* are grown for their foliage.

The two flowering *Plectranthus* that we grow each have their unique characteristics. *Plectranthus hilliardiae* looks like elegant candelabras and has an almost mystical quality about it. The pale lavender, tubular blossoms speckled with deep lavender markings glitter magically in the sunlight. Much like a crystal prism, the multi-faceted form is a source of constant fascination. Adding to the splendor, it blooms nine months of the year and is most closely related to the Swedish ivy in form and growth.

Plectranthus fruiticosa is a vigorous, upright grower that brings forth prolific blooms during the cooler months. Soft pink spires reach up from a circular stage of bronze-toned foliage. We use it to bring an outstanding boost of color to the potted garden during the transition from summer to fall.

the plants

Plumbago

Creating bursts of bloom in a never-ending succession, Plumbagos brightness of color brings meaning and fullness to our world.

BOTANICAL NAME: *Plumbago (plum-bah´-go)*

COMMON NAME: *Cape Leadwort, Scarlet Leadwort*

FAMILY NAME: *Plumbaginaceae*

ORIGIN: *Southeast Asia, South Africa*

LIGHT: *full sun*

SIZE AND GROWTH: *2 - 4 feet in container*
- *P. indica: upright growth habit*
- *P. auriculata: sprawling*

MINIMUM TEMPERATURE:
- *P. indica: 60°F*
- *P. auriculata: 40°F*

BLOOMING SEASON:
- *P. indica: fall and winter; everbloomer*
- *P. auriculata: spring, summer and fall*

OUTSIDE HARDINESS ZONE: *zone 10 and higher*

SOIL: *any well-drained potting mix*

FERTILIZER: *moderate levels of fertilizer year-round as long as temperatures are above 60°F*

BEST TIME TO PRUNE:
- *P. indica: May or June after flowering*
- *P. auriculata: fall or early winter*

PESTS OR DISEASE TO WATCH FOR:
- *insects: occasional susceptibility to aphids and mealy bugs*
- *foliar disease: none*
- *root disease: none*

UNIQUE CHARACTERISTICS/OTHER GROWING TIPS:

Plumbago indica has an unusual flowering habit. For weeks, the flower spike continues to bloom in an upward fashion leaving bare stems behind. Although it has an upright habit, the stems often need some staking. *Plumbago auriculata* has a long period of bloom, works well outside as a summer container plant, and is a fast grower. It also can be trained into a standard where its arching branches, floriferous in nature, create beautiful specimens. *Plumbagos* are enduring plants and can be grown for years in the same pot. They welcome the cycle of growth, bloom, hard pruning and back into growth again. We often grow *Plumbagos* for display plants because they are reliable bloomers from spring through

Plumbago indica

Above left: Plumbago auriculata 'Imperial Blue'; right: Plumbago auriculata alba

fall. Prune them hard in late fall when the flowers are waning, then move them to a warm, sunny spot, preferably above 60°F. They immediately begin growth again and by mid-winter are back in bud.

Plumbagos are fast growing, colorful plants that accent any home or garden. At Logee's, we grow four varieties of *Plumbago*. *Plumbago auriculata* has three different colors. We grow the alba, or white colored form, and two blue varieties. *P.*

auriculata 'Imperial Blue' is an attractive, deep blue color that blooms in typical phlox-like clusters. The *P. auriculatas* are sprawling in form and make lovely basket plants.

The bases of the flowers have a sticky substance on them and we can always tell when a grower has pruned the *Plumbagos*. More noticeable than being tarred with feathers, they unconsciously walk around with attractive blue petals

attached to their shirt, pants and hair.

Plumbago indica is also a lovely variety, nicely named "Scarlet Leadwort." This winter flowering plant with its soft red, festive colors is a nice change from the traditional poinsettias during the holidays. It flowers from December to June.

the plants

Porphyrocoma

Cheeriness is found in the blossoms, for wherever it grows the essence of its beauty is revealed.

BOTANICAL NAME: *Porphyrocoma pohliana (por-fiˊ-row-ko-ma)*
COMMON NAME: *Rose Pinecone*
FAMILY NAME: *Acanthaceae*
ORIGIN: *South America*
LIGHT: *partial sun to shade*
SIZE AND GROWTH: *6 to 10 inches in container; upright growth habit*
MINIMUM TEMPERATURE: *50°F*
BLOOMING SEASON: *everbloomer*
HARDINESS ZONE: *zone 10 and higher*
SOIL: *any well-drained potting mix*
FERTILIZER: *low to moderate levels of fertilizer applied year-round; if grown in shade, reduce fertilizer; if grown in full sun, increase fertilizer*
BEST TIME TO PRUNE: *anytime*
PESTS OR DISEASE TO WATCH FOR:
• *insects: some susceptibility to mealy bug*
• *foliar disease: some susceptibility under cold, damp conditions, botrytis*
• *root disease: none*

UNIQUE CHARACTERISTICS/ OTHER GROWING TIPS:

Rose Pinecone produces seeds very easily. The seedpods snap and the seeds pop out. Many have escaped into the greenhouses and we find new plants growing under benches, even where light levels are low. Propagation can be done by seed or cutting. If kept under full sun, the foliage will get brassy and hard looking. Keep in partial sun to shade for best results.

We've had Rose Pinecone in the greenhouses for about twenty years. Its colorful bracts appear year-round, even under low light conditions. As soon as one bloom fades, another quickly re-sprouts. Each flower lasts several weeks, which makes it a free-blooming plant. Its colorful bracts are not the only attraction. Rose Pinecone has outstanding var-iegated silver leaves and only reaches modest heights, which makes it good for windowsill or tabletop culture.

Porphyrocoma pohliana

Prostanthera

A multitude of blooms comes forth from its presence, heralding the birth of a new season.

Prostanthera saxicola 'Montana'

BOTANICAL NAME: *Prostanthera* (pros-tanth-e´-ra)
COMMON NAME: *Australian Mint Bush*
FAMILY NAME: *Labiatae*
ORIGIN: *Australia*

LIGHT: *full sun*
SIZE AND GROWTH:
- *P. asplathoides: 1½ feet*
- *P. incisa rosea: 1½ feet*
- *P. nivea: 3 - 5 feet*
- *P. saxicola: 5 inches in container*

MINIMUM TEMPERATURE: *35°F; grow cold to insure flowering*
BLOOMING SEASON: *late winter and spring*
OUTSIDE HARDINESS ZONE: *zone 9 and higher*
SOIL: *any well-drained potting mix*
FERTILIZER: *low levels of fertilizer applied year-round except wintertime; problems arise if they are made to grow too fast with excessive amounts of fertilizer*
BEST TIME TO PRUNE: *immediately after flowering*
PESTS OR DISEASE TO WATCH FOR:
- *insects: none*
- *foliar disease: none*
- *root disease: some susceptibility to root rots if grown under high fertility with damp conditions*

UNIQUE CHARACTERISTICS/OTHER GROWING TIPS:

These winter-blooming bushes have one thing in common: their flowers bloom en masse during the flowering cycle. One area that needs to be addressed is the problem with "Sudden Death Syndrome" (SDS). *P. nivea* is a strong grower but the other varieties are susceptible to SDS. When these mint bushes are over-fertilized, root disease often gets in and takes over. Then the damaged roots can no longer take up water and suddenly, without warning, they collapse. *Prostantheras* will take some freezing temperatures. We like to grow them in clay pots in a cool, sunny spot and grow them a little under potted, as they can handle dry conditions better than wet. Flowers form during the cool nights of fall and early winter. Once flowering begins, the cooler the temperature, the longer the flowering cycle will last. With the exception of *P. nivea*, the varieties we grow are compact to dwarf, making them perfect for windowsill culture.

PLEASE NOTE: severe prunings are often not received well. Prune regularly as the plant develops, rather than waiting until it has gotten out of hand.

the plants

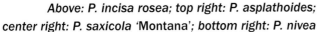

*Above: P. incisa rosea; top right: P. asplathoides;
center right: P. saxicola 'Montana'; bottom right: P. nivea*

These Australian mint bushes add wonderful fragrance to any herb garden. Their foliage has an enticing, pungent aroma. *P. incisa rosea* is especially noted for its bright pink flowers that literally smother the foliage in late winter. *P. asplathoides* is a dwarf mint bush that is also aromatic but not as showy with the blooms. Yet when the flowering cycles are complete, their fragrance continues to fill the growing space year-round.

Two *Prostantheras* that we grow, *P. nivea* and *P. saxicola* 'Montana' are not fragrant but each has unique aspects. *P. Nivea* has large flowers with needle-like leaves; it smothers itself in blooms in late spring. *P. saxicola* is dwarf and makes an excellent hanging basket or bonsai.

prostanthera

Pseuderanthemum

In all its glory, Amethyst Star shines forth in great abundance.

BOTANICAL NAME:
Pseuderanthemum (soo-de´-ranth-e-mum) 'Amethyst Star'
COMMON NAME: *Amethyst Star*
FAMILY NAME: *Acanthaceae*
ORIGIN: *unknown*

LIGHT: *full to partial sun*
SIZE AND GROWTH: *12 - 20 inches in container; upright growth habit*
MINIMUM TEMPERATURE: *55°F*

BLOOMING SEASON: *late summer, fall and early winter; intermittently throughout the year*
OUTDOOR HARDINESS ZONE: *zone 10 and higher*
SOIL: *any well-drained potting mix*
FERTILIZER: *low to moderate amounts of fertilizer applied from spring to fall, as long as temperatures are above 60°F*
BEST TIME TO PRUNE: *after flowering cycle; in early spring*
PESTS OR DISEASE TO WATCH FOR:
- *insects: occasional aphids*
- *foliear disease: none*
- *root disease: none*

UNIQUE CHARACTERISTICS/OTHER GROWING TIPS:

To grow 'Amethyst Star' well, prune immediately after the flowering cycle and not again. Also, to insure flowering, grow plant tight in container and do not over fertilize. It is an unreliable bloomer if pushed too hard with excessive amounts of fertilizer. Light levels are another factor for flowering. Part of the day, they need direct sunlight, preferably in a south or east window. We recommend a high phosphate feed quarterly, which helps to boost blossoms. To create a thick, full specimen, prune symmetrically. Their upright growth habit tends to produce branches that reach outward from the main plant.

We use this upright grower to bring a splash of color to our displays during late summer and fall. However, we also find it sporadically blooming throughout the year. When cultured properly, the shortening day length brings blooms en masse. Often the branches will have so many flowers present that the foliage disappears. This cultivar boasts unusual raspberry-colored blooms in the shape of stars. The bright and inviting color reminds us of sipping on a raspberry cooler on a hot summer's day. A strong grower and resistance to bugs and disease make this a good candidate for a sunlit spot inside, or for outdoor culture where temperatures permit.

Punica

The Dwarf Pomegranate flowers awaken the essence of rebirth, honoring the seasonal change of spring.

BOTANICAL NAME: *Punica granatum 'Nana' (pew´-ni-ka)*
COMMON NAME:
Dwarf Pomegranate
FAMILY NAME: *Punicaceae*
ORIGIN: *Mediterranean to Himalaya*

LIGHT: *full to partial sun*
SIZE AND GROWTH: *2 feet in container; upright growth habit*
MINIMUM TEMPERATURE: *40°F*
BLOOMING SEASON: *spring and summer*
OUTSIDE HARDINESS ZONE: *zone 8 and higher*
SOIL: *any well-drained soil*
FERTILIZER: *moderate levels of fertilizer during active growth (spring and summer)*
BEST TIME TO PRUNE: *prune back in mid-winter, just before they begin to grow again*
PESTS OR DISEASE TO WATCH FOR:
- *insects: occasional mealy bug*
- *foliar disease: none*
- *root disease: none*

UNIQUE CHARACTERISTICS/OTHER GROWING TIPS:
The Dwarf Pomegranate is deciduous and has a resting period in the late fall and early winter. This simply means that many of their leaves will yellow and drop. They won't begin to grow out again until late winter or early spring. However, under warmer conditions, they don't always drop their leaves. When grown in a pot for many years, they get woody, look like little trees, and become a member of the family.

Dwarf Pomegranates make a wonderful conversation piece. Whether cultured as a bonsai or windowsill plant, these miniature beauties produce small fruit that dangle from their woody branches. We find the fruit to be somewhat sour; however, if grown under enough light, the sweetness will be enhanced. This enduring plant grows for many years in the same pot without the need for transplanting. The older and woodier they become, the more impressive their presence.

Not only is this Dwarf Pomegranate praised for the fruit, its flowers are indeed a treat to behold. The beautiful orange blooms hang like bells from loosely foliated stems. Propagation can be done by seed or cutting. Children especially love to open the fruit, stare in awe at all the little red seeds, then plant as many as possible in a container. This variety makes an unusual school project that gets even the least interested child involved.

Rondeletia

An intricacy of fragrance held within each cluster awakens a peaceful remembrance.

BOTANICAL NAME: *Rondeletia (ron-del-lee´-sha) splendens*
COMMON NAME: *Panama Rose*
FAMILY NAME: *Rubiaceae*
ORIGIN: *Central America*

LIGHT: *full sun*
SIZE AND GROWTH:
- *R. splendens: 10 - 16 inches in pot; sprawling growth habit*
- *R. leucophylla: 1 - 3 feet in container; upright growth habit*

MINIMUM TEMPERATURE:
- *R. splendens: 50°F*
- *R. leucophylla: 60°F*

BLOOMING SEASON:
- *R. splendens: everbloomer*
- *R. leucophylla: winter and spring*

OUTSIDE HARDINESS ZONE: *zone 10 and higher*
SOIL: *any well-drained potting mix*
FERTILIZER: *moderate amounts of fertilizer year-round as long as temperatures are above 60°F*
BEST TIME TO PRUNE:
- *R. splendens: anytime*
- *R. leucophylla: after blooming (late spring to early summer)*

PESTS OR DISEASE TO WATCH FOR:
- *insects: some susceptibility to mealy bug*
- *foliar disease: none*
- *root disease: R. leucophylla has some susceptibility to root rot during the wintertime when temperatures are cold and light levels are low*

UNIQUE CHARACTERISTICS/OTHER GROWING TIPS:

R. splendens does well as a basket plant or anywhere a plant is needed to cascade over container edges as it displays its sprawling, arching form. *R. leucophylla*, a reliable seasonal bloomer from December to June, is also noted for its abundance of sweet-scented flowers. Periodically, every year or two, both varieties benefit from a hard pruning. As severe as it seems, this involves removing two-thirds of the growth; they quickly sprout back, creating a much fuller specimen. Do this when they're in their active growth of late spring or early summer. Although both make good potted plants for a sunny location, *R. leucophylla* can experience leaf drop during the winter. This is usually related to root diseases brought on by cool temperatures and low light. The plant generally does not die from this root disease but growth does look unsightly. When grown in clay pots with temperatures kept above 65°F, root disease problems are reduced.

The two varieties of *Rondeletias* that we grow are *R. leucophylla*, a short day bloomer, and *R. splendens*, an everbloomer. At first, we only thought *R. leucophylla* had an evening fragrance. However, one mid-summer's evening many years ago, we happened to be in the greenhouse around midnight and an intense sandalwood smell permeated the air. As we traced it, the scent belonged to *R. splendens*. We had grown *R. splendens* for years and never knew about its mysterious evening scent. Strangely enough, the fragrance only comes out very late at night and does not always emit such a

powerful scent. Regardless of its fragrance, umbells of rose-red blooms on upright stems create a never-ending display of color that makes *R. splendens* a popular choice for basket and pot culture.

Left: Rondeletia splendens;
above: Rondeletia leucophylla

rondeletia

Ruellia

Magnetizing the senses, Ruellia's brilliant color awakens the heart to the depths of love.

BOTANICAL NAME: *Ruellia*
(roo-el´-ee-a)
COMMON NAME: *Christmas Pride, Trailing Velvet*
FAMILY NAME: *Acanthaceae*
ORIGIN: *Brazil, South America*

LIGHT:
- *R. makoyana: full sun to shade*
- *R. macrantha and R. Elegans: full sun*

SIZE AND GROWTH:
- *R. elegans: 8 inches; scandant growth habit*
- *R. makoyana: 12 inches; scandant growth habit*
- *R. macrantha: 2 - 3 feet; upright growth habit*

MINIMUM TEMPERATURE: *50°F*
BLOOMING SEASON:
- *R. elegans: everbloomer*
- *R. makoyana and R. macrantha: fall and winter*

OUTSIDE HARDINESS ZONE: *zone 10 and higher*
SOIL: *any well-drained potting mix*
FERTILIZER: *moderate levels of fertilizer applied year-round as long as temperatures are above 60°F*

BEST TIME TO PRUNE: *after flowering cycle is complete*
PESTS OR DISEASE TO WATCH FOR:
- *insects: some susceptibility to white fly, aphids and spider mite*
- *foliar disease: none*
- *root disease: none*

UNIQUE CHARACTERISTICS/OTHER GROWING TIPS:
Short day bloomers, such as *R. macrantha* and *R. makoyana* are fast growers and easy to cultivate as long as the light levels are adequate. *R. elegans* flowers year-round

Facing page: R. makoyana; above: R. macrantha; right: R. elegans

with flowers held high above the foliage on slender stems. For *R. macrantha* to flower well, it must obain some height. Also, do not prune any later than early summer. Give full to partial sun and buds will form in the fall. After the flowering cycle is finished, prune several times to create multiple stems. As winter comes again, upward growth stops as it puts out waves of heavy bloom. *R. macrantha* is a showy plant with large flowers. It tolerates cool nights.

Ruellias are grown for their brilliant flowers. From the everbloomer, *R. elegans*, to the winter bloomers, such as *R. macrantha* and *R. Makoyana*, their colorful floral show is outstanding. *R. elegans* and *R. makoyana* make great basket plants because of their lateral or scandant growth habit. Also, *R. makoyana* has dense branching foliage, which fills out a pot, creating a full specimen with ease. We especially like *R. makoyana* for its year-round decorative, silver-veined foliage.

R. macrantha, on the other hand, is not compact but quite tall, having an upright habit that is extenuated by its long internodes. Therefore, when plants are young, prune back growth several times to create a multiple-stemmed specimen.

Russellia

A soft gentleness resides in the arching stems, yet displays fullness and strength.

BOTANICAL NAME: *Russellia* (rus-el´-ee-a)

COMMON NAME: *Coral Plant, Fountain Plant*

FAMILY NAME: *Scrophulariaceae*

ORIGIN: *Central America, Cuba, Columbia, Mexico*

Russellia sarmentosa

LIGHT: *full sun*

SIZE AND GROWTH: *12 inches in container; upright to weeping growth habit*

MINIMUM TEMPERATURE: *55°F*

BLOOMING SEASON: *everbloomer; peaks in the summer*

OUTSIDE HARDINESS ZONE: *zone 10 and higher*

SOIL: *any well-drained potting mix*

FERTILIZER: *moderate amounts of fertilizer year-round, except under cool conditions below 60°F*

BEST TIME TO PRUNE: *anytime growth is excessive*

PESTS OR DISEASE TO WATCH FOR:
- *insects: R. equisetiformis has occasional susceptibility to mealy bug; R. sarmentosa has some susceptibility to mealy bug, aphids, spider mite*
- *foliar disease: none*
- *root disease: none*

UNIQUE CHARACTERISTICS/ OTHER GROWING TIPS:

Russellias are rapid growers and easy to culture. They can be used outside for summer containers or indoors for a colorful show. To get *Russellias* to flower well, make sure you give them plenty of sunlight.

Russellias make excellent plants for basket or container culture. The two varieties that we grow at Logee's each have their unique characteristics. *R. sarmentosa* has slender arching stems and delicate pointed leaves, which add to their weeping, cascading habit. Their red flowers form on the growing tips, giving a fountain-like effect, hence its common name, Fountain Plant.

R. equisitesformis is similar in form; however, its leafless stems and branches create a needle-like effect that is dense and full. Red flowers dangle from the cascading growth and in frost-free areas make an excellent landscaping plant. Overall, *Russellias* are fast growers and easy to culture. When they are placed outside in the summertime in pots, gracing patios and entryways, a breathtaking atmosphere is created.

The richness of these pastel tones sustains the relationship between plant and man that is felt deep within the soul and delights the heart.

BOTANICAL NAME: *Salvia* (sal´-vee-a)

COMMON NAME: *Sage*

FAMILY NAME: *Labiatae*

ORIGIN: *Central and South America*

LIGHT: *full sun*

SIZE AND GROWTH: *see chart; upright growth habit, some are trailing*

MINIMUM TEMPERATURE: *most to 35°F; some will tolerate freezing*

BLOOMING SEASON: *heaviest blooming in summer; depends on variety; see chart*

OUTSIDE HARDINESS ZONE: *zone 8 - 10 and higher; S. officinale will go into zone 5*

SOIL: *any well-drained potting mix*

FERTILIZER: *moderate levels of fertilizer from spring to fall, or continuous if under high light and warm temperatures year-round*

BEST TIME TO PRUNE: *after flowering cycle is complete for seasonal bloomers; do not prune fall bloomers after June 1; prune everbloomers in late winter or spring, or when flowering is at its lowest*

PESTS OR DISEASE TO WATCH FOR:

• *insects: high susceptibility to white fly; moderate susceptibility to spider mite and aphids*

• *foliar disease: botrytis under cool conditions (flowers and foliage both susceptible)*

• *root disease: some susceptibility under damp conditions*

UNIQUE CHARACTERISTICS/OTHER GROWING TIPS:

Salvias are most effectively used in containers, garden borders, sunrooms and southern windows. Fall blooming varieties need to be brought indoors before the frost season. In temperate areas, *Salvias* are used as container plants for sunny growing spaces. When *Salvias* start out as young cuttings, they need to be pinched to create multiple-stemmed specimens. We often pot three cuttings per pot to quickly create a full container. Starting in February or March with young plants, we are rewarded

S. guaranitica 'Black and Blue

with flowering containers by summertime.

Some of the summer blooming *Salvias* can be planted directly into the ground. For fall bloomers, start with young cuttings; pinch them

salvia

*Left: S. greggii 'Rasberry Royal';
below: S. coccinea 'Peach'*

back, preferably twice before the first of June. Then, allow them to grow until flowering. After blooming cycle, prune them back hard. They will sprout out quickly and can then be maintained until the next summer season.

Another possibility, which we prefer, is to propagate new plants from the old one. This gives a fresh start and reduces the room taken up during the winter by the old, large plants. They easily root from cutting. If grown without much

fertilizer, they will maintain a limited size until potted up again in late spring.

Avoid excessive dampness when growing *S. chamaedryoides*, whose sprawling habit and silvery foliage is an eye-catcher.

the plants

NAME	SIZE	BLOOMING SEASON
S. chamaedryoides	8 - 10 inches	summer
S. discolor	16 - 30 inches	summer
S. elegans	16 - 24 inches	fall
S. guaranitica	2 feet	spring, summer, fall
S. guaranitica 'Black and Blue'	2 feet	spring, summer, fall
S. 'Indigo Spires'	2 - 3 feet	summer, fall
S. leucantha	2 - 3 feet	fall
S. officinale 'Berggarten'	12 - 18 inches	shy bloomer
S. officinale 'Purpurascens'	16 - 20 inches	summer
S. 'Purple Majesty'	2 feet	spring, summer, fall
S. sinaloensis	12 - 18 inches	summer, fall
S. van houtti	2 - 3 feet	summer, fall

There are more than nine hundred species of *Salvias*. From flowering sages to aromatic and culinary sages, this family is a must for every garden. Some Salvias are hardy in the northern zones. Some are used as annuals, while others are tender perennials used for seasonal color throughout the year as potted plants or grown in seasonal flowerbeds. At Logee's, we grow over two dozen varieties, most tropical or subtropical. They are fast and easy to grow, need high light levels, and boast exquisite shades of color for the summer garden.

S. officinale is a heavily aromatic cooking sage. Some of the most brilliant varieties are as follows. *S. guaranitica* 'Black and Blue' is a three-season bloomer with blue-violet blooms. *S. leucantha* has a spectacular show of lavender flowers for fall and early winter. The *greggii* cultivars like 'Raspberry Royal' make superb potted plants as well as garden favorites because of their modest height.

Many of the blooming varieties have aromatic foliage, which adds to their charm. *S. elegans* is the famous 'Pineapple Sage', with pineapple-scented foliage and brilliant red flowers that bloom in the fall. *S. coccinea* 'Peach' is a wonderful free-blooming cultivar that smothers itself in pastel salmon flowers from spring through fall.

S. chamaedryoides

salvia

135

Scutellaria

Blooming year-round, power and passion shine forth as a statement of intense brilliance.

BOTANICAL NAME: *Scutellaria* (sku-te-lah´-ree-a)
COMMON NAME: *Skull Cap*
FAMILY NAME: *Labiatae*
ORIGIN: *Costa Rica, China*

LIGHT: *full to partial sun*
SIZE AND GROWTH: *1 - 2 feet in container; upright to spreading growth habit*
MINIMUM TEMPERATURE:
- *S. costaricana: 60°F*
- *S. formosana: 35°F*
- *S. suffrutescens: 35°F*

BLOOMING SEASON: *everbloomers with high light levels; generally, S. formosana and S. suffrutescens are summer bloomers because winter light is not strong enough*
OUTSIDE HARDINESS ZONE:
- *S. costaricana: zone 10*
- *S. formosana: zone 7*
- *S. suffrutescens: zone 8*

SOIL: *any well-drained potting mix*
FERTILIZER: *moderate amounts of fertilizer year-round except if grown below 60°F*
BEST TIME TO PRUNE:
- *S. costaricana: anytime growth is excessive*

Scutellaria formosana

- *S. formosana and S. suffrutescens: winter or early spring*

PESTS OR DISEASE TO WATCH FOR:
- *insects: moderate susceptibility to white fly, spider mite and aphids*
- *foliar disease: S. Costaricana has some susceptibility to botrytis*
- *root disease: none*

UNIQUE CHARACTERISTICS/OTHER GROWING TIPS:

Older plants of *S. costaricana* need staking. They often get scraggly or loose looking; therefore, we recommend a severe pruning. They will quickly re-sprout and reward the gardener with magnificent blooms.

the plants

Left: Scutellaria costricana;
below: Scutellaria suffrutescens

S. suffrutescens occasionally show signs of iron chlorosis when grown cold during the winter. Grow on the dry side with high light levels to avoid the disease.

We grow five varieties of *Scutellaria* at Logee's. Medicinally, Skullcap is known for its pain relieving properties. Skullcap has been reported to relieve even the worst headache and produces a relaxing effect when taken internally.

Besides their medicinal qualities,

Scutellarias are very showy plants. *S. costaricana* is a reliable bloomer for year-round display and color. Its unique ability to re-flower off the same flower stem is distinctive in the world of plants. In other words, the mileage you get from one bloom is astounding.

S. formosana, on the other hand, does not have the extended blooming cycle that *S. costaricana* does. However, during its flowering season, it's a heavy bloomer. We like *S. formosana* because it makes an

excellent garden plant or outdoor container plant in milder areas and becomes a full, bushy specimen.

S. suffretescens is a dwarf Scutellaria compared to other varieties. Rarely growing over one foot in height, its small stature becomes bushy and gets smothered in little pink flowers. We often recommend this variety for the limited space gardener.

scutellaria

Senecio

Reflections of light and joy are seen in the wandering brightness of this floral display.

BOTANICAL NAME: *Senecio*
(se-ne´-kee-o)
COMMON NAME: *Orangeglow Vine*
FAMILY NAME: *Compositae*
ORIGIN: *Mexico*

LIGHT: *full sun*
SIZE AND GROWTH: *12 inches in container; vining in habit*
MINIMUM TEMPERATURE: *45°F*
BLOOMING SEASON: *spring, summer, fall*
OUTSIDE HARDINESS ZONE: *zone 10 and higher*
SOIL: *any well-drained potting mix*
FERTILIZER: *moderate amounts of fertilizer from spring to fall*
BEST TIME TO PRUNE: *preferably winter to spring, but can be pruned any time*
PESTS OR DISEASE TO WATCH FOR:
* *insects: high susceptibility to aphids; some susceptibility to white fly and mealy bug*
    * *foliar disease: none*
    * *root disease: none*

UNIQUE CHARACTERISTICS/OTHER GROWING TIPS:
S. confusus is a climbing vine that

works well as a basket plant. It flowers best when given the high light of summer. If they don't flower, check the light levels. They need full sun. As rapid growers, they are favored as annuals in summer containers. For full pots, we recommend three or more plants. They freely come into bloom during late summer.

Senecios have brilliant orange flowers and have appropriately been coined the "Orangeglow Vine." These fast growers make

Facing page: S. confusus 'Sao Paulo'; above: S. confusus

wonderful basket displays or container plants because of their ability to sprawl over the edge. *S. confusus* has a delightful fragrance, which is especially noticed on a sunny day. *S. confusus* 'Sao Paulo' is not fragrant but is a heavier, vigorous grower that produces spectacular blooms nonetheless.

In the summertime, when they are in bloom, Senecios growth habit is more trailing than climbing. They are not aggressive twining vines, but like to ramble along supports such as fences or lattice walls. We especially like to use these daisy-like flowers in mixed container plantings in the summertime. To see an orange daisy is unusual and always seems to inspire all that pass.

senecio

Solandra

Welcoming and wonderful, these fragrant flowers initiate expansion into the realm of what is possible.

BOTANICAL NAME: *Solandra*
COMMON NAME: *Golden Chalice*
FAMILY NAME: *Solanaceae*
ORIGIN: *Caribbean, New World Tropics*

LIGHT: *full sun*
SIZE AND GROWTH: *2 - 4 feet in container; vining in habit*
MINIMUM TEMPERATURE: *45°F*
BLOOMING SEASON: *fall, winter*
OUTSIDE HARDINESS ZONE: *zone 10 and higher*
SOIL: *any well-drained potting mix*
FERTILIZER: *moderate levels of fertilizer from spring to fall*
BEST TIME TO PRUNE: *immediately after flowering; important to give a hard pruning at that time*
PESTS OR DISEASE TO WATCH FOR:
- *insects: high susceptibility to aphids; moderate susceptibility to white fly*
- *foliar disease: none*
- *root disease: none*

UNIQUE CHARACTERISTICS/OTHER GROWING TIPS:

Prune *Solandras* after their flowering cycle and then do not prune again. If pruned too late, *Solandras* will not flower for the next season. Therefore, the challenge is — How to maintain the plant in a pot with such a vigorous growth habit?

Solandras put out big, thick, heavy stems. To maintain *Solandras*, the trick is to prune them hard enough so the size of the container and growing room will hold the plant for the remainder of the year.

PLEASE NOTE: Their heavy vines do need support. Also, to help maintain the plant, we recommend taking the leads, or vining growths, and wrapping them around themselves. Tie to stakes or bend the vining stem and then tie it to a support. When grown in tropical areas, the shear weight of these heavy vines will take down an eight- to ten-inch diameter tree. When planted directly into the ground, they become huge, massive mounds of foliage and make an excellent privacy screen.

Another trick to get *Solandras* to flower is to give them blossom-boosting fertilizer, which contains high phosphate levels. During active growth, give blossom-boosting fertilizer every two weeks. *Solandras* make a huge statement and are especially welcomed by the

S. longiflora; facing page: S. maxima variegated

gardener with lots of space.

Have you ever seen such a wonder? Immense flowers in the shape of a chalice have an open-mouth bloom reaching six to eight inches across. And to top it off, the two *Solandras* that we grow, *S. maxima* and *S. longiflora*, are fragrant. They are heavy growing vines that delight the senses with their blend of white colors that deepen to a rich, golden-yellow with age. Both respond to the shortening day length of summer to initiate bloom. By the time fall arrives, the flowering cycle has begun, lasting well into the winter months.

We also grow a variegated form of *S. maxima*. Not only are the flowers magnificent to behold but the foliage is as well. When the leaves are young, the foliage has an unusual purple tinge, adding to any patio garden's splendor.

Growing vigorously all summer, buds form on the growing tips with the decreasing day length. Therefore, pruning at the right time is critical to create a full, bushy specimen. We recommend pruning immediately after the flowering cycle. As a vine, pruning is necessary to encourage shape and form.

solandra

Stapelia

The manifestation of Starfish Flower brings a deeper understanding of life's creative forces.

Stapelia gigantea

BOTANICAL NAME: *Stapelia gigantea (sta-peel-e´-a)*
COMMON NAME: *Starfish Flower*
FAMILY NAME: *Asclepiadacea*
ORIGIN: *South Africa*

LIGHT: *full to partial sun*
SIZE AND GROWTH: *10 - 12 inches in container; upright growth habit*
MINIMUM TEMPERATURE: *40°F*
BLOOMING SEASON: *summer, fall*

OUTSIDE HARDINESS ZONE: *zone 10 and higher*
SOIL: *cactus soil or any well-drained potting mix*
FERTILIZER: *low to moderate levels of fertilizer during the summer; do not fertilize during the winter*
BEST TIME TO PRUNE: *winter or early spring.*
PESTS OR DISEASE TO WATCH FOR:
• *insects: low susceptibility to mealy bug*
• *foliar disease: none, unless grown under high humidity and continuous dampness*
• *root disease: none, except under high moisture, damp soil conditions*

UNIQUE CHARACTERISTICS/OTHER GROWING TIPS:
No mistaking this one. True to its name, Starfish Flower is actually bigger than most ocean starfish. Its fat green stems are succulent and sharply angled. And although the stems look cactus-like, there are no thorns to worry about. The flower itself is an unusual, immense size. Reaching nine inches across in diameter, the subdued-yellow, star-shaped flower is covered by miniature purple hairs.

S. gigantea is a most unusual plant that requires little care. Its upright stems spread, with new shoots coming out of the growing base like a rhizome. This unique characteristic makes *S. gigantea* a full, thick succulent with flowers emerging off the sides of the stems.

Much like the Night Blooming Cereus, *S. gigantea* flowers in waves throughout the summer and fall until its blooming cycle is complete. Going through cycles of bloom, half a dozen buds will open, then diminish. The plant will put on more growth, and then bloom again. When pruning, only remove the outer stems to bring the plant back to size. Stapelia makes a good hanging basket because its stems often trail over the edge.
PLEASE NOTE: The down side to growing this variety is its odor. This plant smells like rotting meat and is best enjoyed from a distance. The scent does attract flies, which pollinate the plant.

the plants

Stephanotis

A flower that celebrates the union of spirit and love.

BOTANICAL NAME: *Stephanotis floribunda (ste-fa-no´-tis)*
COMMON NAME: *Madagascar Jasmine*
FAMILY NAME: *Asclepiadacea*
ORIGIN: *Madagascar*

LIGHT: *full to partial sun*
SIZE AND GROWTH: *2 - 3 feet in container; vining in habit*
MINIMUM TEMPERATURE: *50°F*
BLOOMING SEASON: *spring, summer*
OUTSIDE HARDINESS ZONE: *zone 10 and higher*
SOIL: *any well-drained potting mix*
FERTILIZER: *moderate levels of fertilizer applied from spring to fall, or during active growth*
BEST TIME TO PRUNE: *winter*
PESTS OR DISEASE TO WATCH FOR:
• *insects: high susceptibility to mealy bug*
• *foliar disease: none*
• *root disease: none as long as not kept excessively damp during cool weather*

UNIQUE CHARACTERISTICS/OTHER GROWING TIPS:

As a mature plant, *Stephanotis* has a resting period in the winter when growth stops. However, a young cutting will continue to grow. After, its semi-dormancy, in late February, it begins to grow again. New shoots form off the old vine and flower buds initiate at the leaf axis along the stem. Flowers open during the summer. Buds will continue to initiate until late summer, then the process begins to slow down.

One of the biggest complaints we get is "Why doesn't my *Stephanotis* flower at home?" We recommend the following to enhance flowering. Give them consistent and moderate levels of fertilizer. We also recommend high phosphate feed or blossom boosting feed, interchanged with balanced fertilizer throughout the season. Give them direct sunlight either in the morning or the afternoon and allow a period of dryness between waterings. Be sure there is a temperature differential of ten to

Stephanotis floribunda

fifteen degrees between day and night. In no time, fragrant flowers will reward you.

For years, this Madagascar Jasmine has been known for its use as a cut flower in weddings. Its fragrance is rich, heavy and intoxicating, setting the matrimonial stage for years of happiness. The virginal white flowers are thick and waxy. Its growth habit is closely related to the Hoya.

Stephanotis has twining vines and shiny leaves, which need support. It makes a wonderful,

stephanotis

fragrant topiary wreath. Supports such as stakes or trellis also work well. Growing up in the greenhouses had its advantages; the Logee-Martin children fondly remember Stephanotis as a big vine that rambled around on the ceiling of one of the older greenhouses. The elders would use Madagascar Jasmine in their cut flower work, but many times they would come up short because the children were a step ahead of them. The kids would climb up onto the trellised ceiling, pick the blossoms, and sip on the blossom stems, which contain sweet nectar.

Stephanotis is also a famous conservatory plant and makes a good houseplant for a sunny window. **PLEASE NOTE:** Seedlings can take several years to begin blooming. But if your young plant was started from a cutting, then it will flower right away in the pot.

Stepanotis floribunda

the plants

Streptocarpus

The brightness and beauty of Cape Primrose give strength and vision to the beholder.

BOTANICAL NAME: *Streptocarpus* (strep-to-kar´-pus)
COMMON NAME: *Cape Primrose*
FAMILY NAME: *Gesneriaceae*
ORIGIN: *Africa*

LIGHT: *partial sun to shade*
SIZE AND GROWTH: *4 - 6 inches in container; upright growth habit*
MINIMUM TEMPERATURE: *50°F*
BLOOMING SEASON: *intermittent bloomers about 10 months of the year; lowest is in winter*
OUTSIDE HARDINESS ZONE: *zone 9 and higher*
SOIL: *any well-drained potting mix*
FERTILIZER: *low to moderate amounts of fertilizer year-round with temperatures above 60°F*
BEST TIME TO PRUNE: *do not prune, groom, or remove damaged leaves; if too big for pot, divide*
PESTS OR DISEASE TO WATCH FOR:
• *insects: moderate susceptibility to mealy bug, cyclamine mite*
• *root disease: susceptible to root rot if grown with excessive moisture*

UNIQUE CHARACTERISTICS/OTHER GROWING TIPS:

Streptocarpus are great plants for low light exposure. They grow well under shady conditions. However, there is a threshold of light needed to stimulate flowers. If plants are not blooming, increase the light.

It is rare to have such intense flower colors in partial sun or shade. Yet *Streptocarpus* rewards the gardener time and again with its rich purple, pleasing pink, blue-lavendar or pure white flowers. The hybrids that we grow can be traced back to South Africa's sub-tropical forest. They not only flower freely for ten months of the year, but they adapt admirably to the home environment.

Preferring lower light levels than many other Gesneriads, they will get sunburned if left in direct, harsh sunlight. The cranberry-pink colors of S. 'Jeanette' are held high on stiff stems above the foliage, while S. 'Lord Fauntleroy' blooms in tight, dark purple clusters with a velvety sheen fit for royalty. S. 'Maasen's White' is one of our oldest hybrids and still has a reputation as a profuse, vigorous bloomer.

Clockwise: Streptocarpus 'Lord Fauntleroy'; S. 'Maasen's White'; S. 'Little Gem'

Stictocardia

The flowers hide beneath the foliage, inviting one to seek its blooms with child-like curiosity.

BOTANICAL NAME: *Stictocardia beraviensis (stik-toe-kar´-dee-a)*
COMMON NAME: *Orange Morning Glory*
FAMILY NAME: *Convolvulaceae*
ORIGIN: *Africa*

LIGHT: *full sun*
SIZE AND GROWTH: *3 - 5 feet in container; vining growth habit*
MINIMUM TEMPERATURE: *60°F*
BLOOMING SEASON: *summer, fall, early winter*
OUTSIDE HARDINESS ZONE: *zone 10 and higher*
SOIL: *any well-drained potting mix*
FERTILIZER: *moderate amounts of fertilizer year-round*
BEST TIME TO PRUNE: *after flowering cycle is complete*
PESTS OR DISEASE TO WATCH FOR:
- *insects: moderate susceptibility to spider mite*
- *foliar disease: none*
- *root disease: none*

UNIQUE CHARACTERISTICS/OTHER GROWING TIPS:

If grown outside, *Stictocardia* will not take freezing temperatures. We recommend taking a cutting to start over again, or prune back hard to its original stems. As a potted plant, it needs to be given enough room to allow it to fill out. If planted outside, it can be lifted and repotted. The foliage is large and needs to grow at least three to four feet to display plant and flowers. For a morning glory, its color is truly unique. To train *Stictocardia* on a stake or trellis, remove suckers that might emerge from the base. This allows the size of the plant to be maintained, and it forces energy into the vining stems that help increase flower production. We recommend twelve- to fourteen-inch pots on a four-foot trellis. A plant of this size will throw off suckers one-half inch in diameter.

Closely related to the morning glory, this rapid grower boasts unique orange blooms. Unlike most morning glories, the leaves are large, measuring approximately six to eight inches across. The vine is heavy and grows rapidly; therefore, support is a must.

Flowers come out in clusters at the leaf axis. Yet because the leaf is so large, one must often hunt for the blooms. Children, of course, love this "I Spy"-type of game, and always seem to count more flowers than we can ever find. Much like a bird nest in the springtime, the flowers nestle in between the leaves in a cozy spot. Blooms are short-lived, only lasting a day, which adds to the delight of our children, because the game is always changing.

We often use *Stictocardia* in our outdoor garden plantings in June. By the end of the summer, it has become an eight-foot vine. When grown in fertile ground with support, its foliage makes a wonderful screen on fences or latticework.

Stictocardia beraviensis

stictocardia

147

Strophanthus

Although sometimes called unusual, unique, or even bizarre, this floral beauty represents the many possibilities within creation itself.

Strophanthus gratus

BOTANICAL NAME: *Strophanthus (stro-fan´-thus)*
COMMON NAME: *Climbing Oleander*
FAMILY NAME: *Apocynaceae*
ORIGIN: *West Africa*

LIGHT: *full sun*
SIZE AND GROWTH: *2 - 3 feet in container; vining in habit*
MINIMUM TEMPERATURE: *60°F*
BLOOMING SEASON:
- *S. preussii: summer*
- *S. gratus: spring*

OUTSIDE HARDINESS ZONE: *zone 10 and higher*
SOIL: *any well-drained potting mix*
FERTILIZER: *moderate amounts of fertilizer except in wintertime; some susceptibility to iron chlorosis*
BEST TIME TO PRUNE:
- *S. preussii: after flowering cycle is complete*
- *S. gratus: late winter or just before spring growth resumes*

PESTS OR DISEASE TO WATCH FOR:
- *insects: none*
- *foliar disease: none*
- *root disease: susceptible to root rot during damp, cool temperatures of winter*

UNIQUE CHARACTERISTICS/OTHER GROWING TIPS:
S. preussii blooms are eye-catching while *S. gratus* catches the senses with its candy-like fragrance. *S. preussii* has a resting period during the depths of winter when growth stops. Many of the leaves may turn yellow and fall off. This is normal and is accentuated by low light levels and cool nighttime temperatures. Do not over water at this time or prune back. Wait until the first signs of new growth in late winter, then prune back summer growth. *S. preussii* can be pruned back hard, which will restructure the form for the coming season.

S. gratus, although not a heavy bloomer, will also shed leaves in winter when stressed with low light levels and cool nighttime temperatures. However, it is important to prune immediately after flowering in early summer so the next year's blooming cycle will come out in abundance. *S. gratus* does better when given full sun.

Although both species are vining in habit and require some staking, we grow them more in the form of upright shrubs. When given hard prunings annually, they respond well and make a nice symmetrical form. Throughout the growing season, it may be necessary to prune off any wandering leads, which help keep the budding specimen intact.

Nothing short of a botanical wonder, *S. preussii* has long tendrils that dangle off the end of the flower. This stiff-stemmed vine needs staking as it matures, and is more contained and adaptable to smaller spaces than *S. gratus*. We first acquired *S. preussii* from the Cornell University Botany department over twenty-five years ago.

S. gratus is a heavier grower with large, broad leaves and thick stems. Although it doesn't bloom as heavily as *S. preussii*, when it does flower in the spring, it has a wonderful, sweet, candy smell, reminding us of carefree days.

Strophanthus preussii

strophanthus

Tabernaemontana

The Flower of Love exudes brilliance, clarity and a delicate sweet fragrance that transforms the heart.

Tabernaemontana divaricata

BOTANICAL NAME:
Tabernaemontana divaricata
(tay-ber-nay´-motan-na)
COMMON NAME: *Butterfly Gardenia, Flower of Love*
FAMILY NAME: *Apocynaceae*
ORIGIN: *India to Thailand*

LIGHT: *full to partial sun*
SIZE AND GROWTH: *2 - 4 feet in container; upright growth*

MINIMUM TEMPERATURE: *55°F*
BLOOMING SEASON: *summer*
OUTSIDE HARDINESS ZONE: *zone 10 and higher*
SOIL: *any well-drained potting mix*
FERTILIZER: *moderate levels of fertilizer during active growth; stop fertilizer in winter; some susceptibility to iron chlorosis*
BEST TIME TO PRUNE: *after dormancy of winter, in early spring*
PESTS OR DISEASE TO WATCH FOR:
- *insects: none*
- *foliar disease: none*
- *root disease: none except in wintertime if kept too wet*

UNIQUE CHARACTERISTICS/OTHER GROWING TIPS:

Tabernaemontanas require high light and warm temperatures to successfully flower. The biggest problem is bud blast. They will literally put out flower buds year-round but will not come into flower until the light levels and temperatures are high enough. They can defoliate in the winter during their resting time, and will not grow again until the days lengthen and the sunlight gets strong enough. There are times during winter when the stems will be nearly bare of leaves and flower buds will still hold on to the growing tips. The plants perform best when the temperatures are warm, the days are long, and the light levels are high. Once they awaken to the increasing day length, they can be pruned hard to help restructure and eliminate the bare stems of winter. They will quickly re-grow and come back into bud and flower.

Known as the Flower of Love or the Butterfly Gardenia, the *Tabernaemontanas* that we grow have a delightful, soft fragrance. Their scent intensifies after dark, captivating the senses further. *T. divaricata* and *T. divaricata grandiflora* are similar in all ways except that *T. d. grandiflora* has larger leaves and flowers.

Although they resemble the gardenia, they are much easier to grow and are not as susceptible to root disease and spider mite. They are prolific bloomers in their season; however, *T. d. grandiflora* is not as profuse as *T. divaricata*.

Thunbergia

Thunbergias awaken and inspire as they climb upward, always reaching for the light.

BOTANICAL NAME: *Thunbergia* (thun-berg´-ee-a)
COMMON NAME: *Blue Skyflower, Skyflower of India*
FAMILY NAME: *Acanthaceae*
ORIGIN: *North India*

LIGHT: *full to partial sun*
SIZE AND GROWTH: *2 - 3 feet in container; vining growth habit; T. erecta: upright growth habit*
MINIMUM TEMPERATURE: *60 °F; T. mysorensis: 40 °F*
BLOOMING SEASON:
• *T. grandiflora, T. mysorensis: fall, winter, spring*
• *T. erecta: spring*
• *T. battiscombei: everbloomer*
OUTSIDE HARDINESS ZONE: *zones 8 - 10 and higher*
SOIL: *any well-drained potting mix*
FERTILIZER: *moderate levels of fertilizer year-round as long as temperatures remain above 60 °F; some susceptibility to iron chlorosis*
BEST TIME TO PRUNE: *immediately after flowering cycle is complete; T. Battiscombei can be pruned anytime growth is excessive*

PESTS OR DISEASE TO WATCH FOR:
• *insects: high susceptibility to spider mite; some susceptibility to white fly*
• *foliar disease: none*
• *root disease: none*

UNIQUE CHARACTERISTICS/OTHER GROWING TIPS:

Thunbergias are vigorous growers and need a steady amount of fertilizer year-round as long as temperatures are warm. *T. grandiflora* likes nighttime temperatures above 60°F, while *T. mysorensis* does better in cooler nighttime temperatures in the 40°F range. This helps stimulate flowering. All varieties can withstand a severe pruning. However, the timing of pruning is crucial so as not to interrupt the next year's blooms. Generally, we recommend pruning after the flowering cycle is complete. *T. erecta* should not be pruned severely any later than summer for next spring's flowers. *T. battiscombei*, an everbloomer, can be pruned four to five inches from the soil anytime growth becomes loose and rangy

Thunbergia battiscombei

looking. With minimal staking, *T. battiscombei* can be maintained as a shrub. It will quickly re-sprout and flower. We find that our display plants can go through three hard prunings a year and still spend most of their time in flower. Do not dry out *Thunbergias* too severely.

thunbergia

Above left: Thunbergia grandiflora; right: T. mysorensis

With a severe wilt, *Thunbergias* are susceptible to leaf drop and also are more susceptible to spider mite.

T. grandiflora is day-length sensitive, making the last date for a hard pruning July or August. This gives the plant plenty of time to regrow and form buds as the days shorten. A vigorous grower, much like *T. mysorensis*, *T. grandiflora* needs continuous encouragement of its wandering vines to maintain form and symmetry. When planted in the ground in a conservatory, or outside in milder climates, they make spectacular climbers. *T. mysorensis'* blooms dangle in long chains with new buds forming, opening, and fading. One flowering stem will bloom for months, growing to a length of ten feet or more.

One of the most outstanding blue flowers that bloom faithfully and fill the living space with splendor during the darkest days of the year is *Thunbergia grandiflora*, also known as the Blue Skyflower. We once saw this grown as a climber in the south, and the ten-foot wall of blue flowers was outstanding. As a container plant, it can easily be trained on a stake or trellis. It's a rapid grower that flowers mainly

the plants

during the winter months from November through May.

T. *mysorensis* is also an attractive variety that does well in cooler nighttime temperatures. Its chain-like flowers pendulate from its vigorous vines, creating a spectacular display when room is available. Another favorite of ours is T. *battiscombei*. We've grown it on a south windowsill for years and, when pruned properly, its shrubby, compact growth habit makes a perfect potted plant. T. *battiscombei* boasts attractive lavender flowers, which come out in abundance year-round. T. *erecta* is a shrub-form of this flowering genus, and puts on a dazzling display of purple trumpet blooms in late spring or early summer. When grown restricted in a container, the size is easily managed.

T. grandiflora alba

thunbergia

Trachelospermum

Within its fragrant flowers and beauty, there is the message that anything is possible.

BOTANICAL NAME:
Trachelospermum asiaticum
(tra-kay-lo-sperm´-um)
COMMON NAME: *Asiatic Jasmine,
Confederate Jasmine*
FAMILY NAME: *Apocynaceae*
ORIGIN: *Japan*

LIGHT: *full to partial sun*
SIZE AND GROWTH: *1 - 2 feet in
container; vining in habit*
MINIMUM TEMPERATURE: *40°F*
BLOOMING SEASON: *spring,
summer*
OUTSIDE HARDINESS ZONE: *zone 8
and higher*
SOIL: *any well-drained potting mix*
FERTILIZER: *low to moderate levels
of fertilizer from early spring to fall*
BEST TIME TO PRUNE: *fall and winter, once growth has stopped*
PESTS OR DISEASE TO WATCH FOR:
• *insects: occasional susceptibility to mealy bug*
• *foliar disease: none*
• *root disease: none*

**UNIQUE CHARACTERISTICS/OTHER
GROWING TIPS:**

Trachelospermums are enduring plants because of their cultural requirements. They only need moderate light levels and are tolerant to neglectful watering. The variety of *T. asiaticum* that we grow is often confused with another plant, also named *T. asiaticum*, which is used as a ground cover in the southern United States. The ground cover *T. asiaticum*, unfortunately, does not flower well. Our *T. asiaticum* was once called *T. mandianum*, and has been reclassified. We recommend this *T. asiaticum* for its ability to produce abundant flowers over several months and its adaptability to the home environment.

Trachelospermums are tolerant and hardy to the stress of indoor culture. Of the five varieties we grow, *Trachelospermum asiaticum* has the longest blooming period and the sweetest scent. The creamy yellow flowers start in early to mid-winter, depending on the temperature, and continue well into the summer.

Trachelospermum jasminoides is called the Confederate Jasmine and blooms with one big surge in the springtime. The white flowers have an enduring quality, but their fragrance is not as sweet as *T. asiaticum's*. Overall, *Trachelospermum* vines make excellent topiaries because of their tight growth habit and ability for the leaves to hold even under drought stress. When they are in bloom, they smother themselves in flowers to the point where the foliage cannot be seen.

Trachelospermum asiaticum

Uncarina

The never-ending display of open-faced blooms expresses of great fortitude and abundance.

BOTANICAL NAME: *Uncarina grandidieri*
COMMON NAME: *Uncarina*
FAMILY NAME: *Pedaliaceae*
ORIGIN: *Madagascar*

LIGHT: *full sun*
SIZE AND GROWTH: *1½ - 3 feet; upright growth habit*
MINIMUM TEMPERATURE: *55°F*
BLOOMING SEASON: *spring, summer, fall*
OUTSIDE HARDINESS ZONE: *zone 10 and higher*
SOIL: *any well-drained potting mix*
FERTILIZER: *moderate amounts of fertilizer from spring to fall; restrict fertilizer in the winter*
BEST TIME TO PRUNE: *late winter; can prune severely as it re-sprouts rapidly*
PESTS OR DISEASE TO WATCH FOR:
 • *insects: high susceptibility to white fly; low susceptibility to spider mite*
 • *foliar disease: none*
 • *root disease: susceptible to root rot if grown too cold*

UNIQUE CHARACTERISTICS/OTHER GROWING TIPS:

Uncarina grandidieri is fast growing and flowers freely under full sun. In summertime, give it ample amounts of water. In winter, during its resting stage, cut down on watering. If too much moisture is kept on the roots during winter, root disease may occur. Grow *Uncarina* in clay pots for a quicker dry down time. To maintain size, we recommend hard prunings. It will sprout out quite rapidly.

Brilliant yellow flowers with dark centers set the blooms of this unusual species apart from many others. Under high light conditions, it flowers freely. *Uncarina grandidieri* is also grown for its woody stems and branches. The twisty, asymmetrical growth habit creates an interesting ornamental form. The trunks get thick and are highly noticeable as the flowers and foliage grow only on the tips of the branches.

An excellent plant for indoor culture, it is tolerant to dry conditions. Yet if grown in cool temperatures and low light, Uncarina can be deciduous, dropping nearly all its leaves. Even under the best of conditions, some leaf drop does occur in wintertime. However, if given a warm sunny spot, it flowers through much of the year, only resting for a month or two in the depths of winter.

Uncarina grandidieri

Vigna

Intriguing and outstanding, this rich floral presence awakens the senses.

BOTANICAL NAME: *Vigna caracalla*
COMMON NAME: *Corkscrew Flower*
FAMILY NAME: *Leguminosae*
ORIGIN: *Tropical South America*

LIGHT: *full sun*
SIZE AND GROWTH: *1 - 3 feet; vining growth habit*
MINIMUM TEMPERATURE: *60 °F*
BLOOMING SEASON: *summer and fall*
OUTSIDE HARDINESS ZONE: *zone 10 and higher*
SOIL: *any well-drained potting mix*
FERTILIZER: *moderate amounts of fertilizer throughout growing season; some susceptibility to iron chlorosis*
BEST TIME TO PRUNE: *in late winter before growth resumes*
PESTS OR DISEASE TO WATCH FOR:
 • *insects: high susceptibility to spider mite*
 • *foliar disease: none*
 • *root disease: some susceptibility to root rot during wintertime*

UNIQUE CHARACTERISTICS/OTHER GROWING TIPS:

Vigna caracalla is an excellent vining plant for trellis or stake. And with a little bit of training, it also makes a nice hanging basket. If necessary, because of limited space or excessive growth, it can be pruned lightly once the flowering cycle is finished in the fall. Keep as much foliage on as is practical during the resting period of winter. In later winter or spring, when growth resumes, prune it back hard. Vigorous growth will shortly resume. In climates where there is an extended fall season, *Vigna* can be planted in the ground outside. During the winter months, growth comes to a halt and many times, leaves yellow and defoliate, especially under cool temperatures. Do not keep excessive moisture on them at this time. Allow some dryness between waterings to keep the root system healthy. Once the days lengthen and temperatures rise, new growth will resume with greater vigor.

As a potted plant, the best specimens are created from plants that are a year or older rather than from young cuttings.

Grown for its intense, rich, fragrant bloom and its unique flower structure, this vining climber forms blooms in tight clusters of white to pink-purple flowers. The spiraled flowers are unique in their color and form. Flowers emerge in late summer and early fall and, under warm greenhouse conditions, *Vigna* will flower in the springtime. During the wintertime, it is normal for *Vigna* to go into a resting period.

PLEASE NOTE: Many times *Vigna* is confused with *Phaseolus*, yet they are very different plants.

Vigna caracalla

vigna

159

Part Four

Plant Care

Pruning

Containers

Pests/Disease

Soils and Fertilizers

Watering

Pruning

- *Young cuttings*

- *Mature plants*

- *Best time to prune*

- *Standard or topiary training*

- *Pruning vines and climbers*

How does one create a full, shapely plant dripping with flowers? Prune, prune, prune. Plants must be pruned in order to bring form and shape to the potted plant. In our experience, many gardeners are timid about taking pruning shears and managing a plant in the pot. Yet, in the long run, this is the only way to create spectacular specimens. And although at first the cuts look severe, be assured the plant will grow back with more vigor and beauty.

Pruning Young Cuttings

Remember every plant started as a young cutting or seedling. This is the time to make a decision. Do you want to create an upright bushy plant? Do you want to create a symmetrical form in the way of a topiary or standard? Is your plant a vining or climbing variety? If so, do you want to train it on a stake, trellis or wire hoop, or simply let the vines run wild?

Questions like these need to be answered before moving on. First, however, you must know a little bit about the plant's growing habit. For example, some varieties will never make standards and others will never be climbers. Plants that make good standards have an upright, easily-branching growth habit with the ability to create a crown on top.

Another option for an upright grower is to create a full and bushy specimen. Therefore, pruning is essential to create multiple stems that will give a mature, full look. Young cuttings or seedlings are often pinched or pruned at the beginning. This initial pruning forces new shoots from the axillary buds, which then form a multiple-stemmed plant. Many plants that we grow always get at least one initial pinch. When we talk about young cuttings, we typically use the term "pinch" instead of "prune" because we literally pinch the growing tip off with our fingers.

Fig 1.1

When the plant gets older, then we "prune" part of the leaf or stem because we need a tool such as a pruning shear to accomplish this task.

When a young plant is 6" - 8" tall, prune low enough to leave approximately four to five axillary buds from the soil's surface. This process is critical because you want multiple stems to form near the soil's surface. If the plant is not pruned close to the surface, then a loose, sprawling specimen will form.

Of course, other factors contribute to creating shape, such as light level, fertilizer, genetics of the plant, and growing conditions. But initially, prune, prune, prune. We

plant care

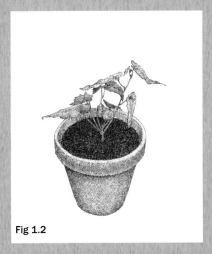
Fig 1.2

Fig 1.3

Fig 1.4

can't stress enough the importance of pruning.

To begin the process, you must be willing to sacrifice the immediate gratification of growth and flowers. However, remember that in the long run, you will create a better specimen. Citrus, Abutilons, Gardenias, Fibrous Begonias, Hibiscus and Clerodendrums are all good examples of pruning young cuttings for spectacular shows later. Brugmansias, or Angel's Trumpets, are an exception to this rule, and need time to grow initially before any cuts are made.

At Logee's, many plants that we grow start their life with an initial cut (Fig. 1.1). The plant will then re-sprout, creating several new shoots (Fig. 1.2) If the plant is a fast grower, we often do one pinch and let it flower. However, another way to create a fuller specimen is to pinch or prune again (Fig. 1.3), allowing the growth to break out and make new stems (Fig. 1.4). If the plant is a slow grower and takes a long time to bloom, such as Citrus or Brunsfelsias, then we recommend two or more initial pinches or prunings. Once the base is thickened with multiple stems, then allow the plant to go through a cycle of growth and bloom. Our famous Pondersosa Lemon needs to have a thickened structure, mainly to bear the heavy fruit, which can weigh five pounds or more.

Pruning Mature Specimens

When is it time to prune a mature specimen? A mature specimen is considered to be mature only after it has gone through a flowering cycle. The size of the pot has nothing to do with its maturity. There is no rule of thumb for pruning mature specimens. Mostly, look at the blooming cycle. Some plants hardly ever need pruning. Others will need a periodic or seasonal pruning to maintain plant size for the container or growing area. Often, pruning will be used simply to restructure a plant.

Best Time to Prune

Generally, prune after a flowering cycle or whenever the plant gets a loose, scraggly appearance. There are several approaches. For the plants that have a seasonal flowering cycle, such as Bouvardia, Clerodendrum, Dichorasandra, Justicia, or Plectranthus, cut back severely once they are out of bloom (Fig. 2.1). Severe pruning means

pruning

163

Fig 2.1

Fig 2.2

Fig 2.3

cutting the plant back to near where the last cuts were made. We remove two-thirds of the plant's growth (Fig. 2.2). This is absolutely necessary to maintain the form. Generally, prune above the leaf node and at the axillary bud. An axillary bud is above a leaf node. These buds are dormant until the cut is made. With a cut, the plant hormones are activated and a new shoot begins to grow. More importantly, excessive growth must be removed, which sometimes means removing all the foliage (Fig. 2.3). The plant will sprout again soon and become fuller.

During the long days of summer or the short days of winter, plants can be pruned, again, depending on their flowering cycle. For example, Dichorisandra comes into full bloom in the fall and will reach anywhere from four to five feet. After its flowering cycle, prune back to one foot from the soil. At this time, a root pruning may need to be done also. Dichorisandra will now grow for another ten months before it is ready to flower again. During the growth period, before flowering, only cut back the unshapely limbs. This minor pruning will keep the plant well groomed until its annual severe

plant care

Fig 3.1

Fig 3.2

pruning. Minor pruning entails pruning the growing tips and stems that look scraggly. Often times, if plants are pruned at the wrong time of the year, they will not flower.

Everbloomers are not as fussy about the timing of pruning. However, to maximize the greatest show of flowers, pay attention to light levels and temperature. Some everbloomers put on glorious shows at certain times of the year, often in the longer day light. After their big show of flowers, they can get scraggly, having leafless limbs and yellow leaves. This is a great time to cut them back severely (Fig. 3.1). We call this a "severe pruning." For example, Abutilons (Flowering Maples) will flower year-round but have a tendency to get leggy looking after a show of flowers. Bringing the plant back into shape after a heavy flowering is an efficient and sensible way to care for the plant (Fig. 3.2).

Anisodontea, Hibiscus, Bouvardia, Abutilon, Pachystachys lutea, and *Pavonia multiflora* are everbloomers and can be pruned at anytime. However, we recommend waiting until after the slow growth of winter. Then, prune them in early spring with the first awakening of growth and vigor. Don't hesitate to prune.

A word of caution — on rare occasions with a severe pruning, the plants don't come back. This rarely happens, but if the plant was already predisposed to a poor root system, the shock of removing all the foliage could kill it.

Another type of pruning is to remove selective leads from slow growers. Plants such as *Murraya paniculta, Michelia figio* and Citrus need only touch up work. Pruning a few growing tips off the mature specimen will thicken growth. Removing selective leads will create a full specimen over many years. We generally don't recommend taking two-thirds of the growth off of slow growers. At the very most, one fourth of the growth may be removed.

pruning

Fig 4.1

Fig 4.2

Fig 4.3

Standard or Topiary Training

Standards and topiaries are trained into a particular structure and are unique, exciting, and challenging. A standard is any plant that has an upright growth habit with a central trunk and a crown of growth on top. A topiary is any plant that is made into a specific form, such as a cone, ball, spiral, bird or elephant. You can make a standard or you can make a standard topiary. In other words, standards have a central stem with a crown on top; if it is formally trained, then it becomes a topiary. At the greenhouses, we grow standards that are either tree-like or formal. Tree-like standards have a central stem and crown. The crown can be upright, or have weeping or cascading branches.

Culturing a plant as a tree-like standard or as a formal topiary brings grace and beauty into any garden space. Good examples of tree-like standards that have a central stem with sprawling or cascading limbs are Brugmansia, Cantua Buxifolia, Lantana, Dombeya, Abutilon, Allamanda, Fibrous Begonia, Crossandra, Hibiscus and Mitriostigma. Not all plants will work, although in theory many should.

How do I know if my plant is a candidate for standard training?

Any plant that has an upright growth habit with short internodes generally makes a good standard, especially when combined with rapid growth. The plant should also have a freely-branching habit, which simply means, once pruned, the stem will give two or more breaks. A formal standard or topi-

plant care

ary needs a tight growth habit as seen in a Myrtle or Rosemary.

Training a tree-like standard or a formal topiary is essentially the same, at first. Start with a young plant that has a straight or central lead. Cut off all other leads that have formed at the base of the plant. Then, pot the plant and allow the specimen to grow to the approximate height that you want the plant to become. Obviously, the taller you want your standard, the longer it will take. However, some varieties must have sufficient heights so they can display their weeping and cascading habits. Trailing Abutilons need to grow anywhere from three to four feet.

During this time of growth, there will be offshoots or side branches coming off the central stem. Cut them off or prune back to encourage the upright growth of the plant. However, do not remove the foliage close to the stem (Fig. 4.1). Leaves create strength and energy, which helps to hasten the overall growth of the plant. It is essential, however, to remove vigorous side branches because then all the plant's energy will be directed into the central stem and force the growth upward. Once the height is obtained, then remove all the side branches except for those on top. Also remove the central lead (Fig.4.2). This will now force the growth below the cut to grow with greater vigor.

There are two different approaches. The first approach requires that you take three, four, or five of the top lateral buds to create the crown. With this structure in place, then start pinching the growth as it rises up. This will create a thickened crown.

The second approach, which we prefer, requires you to pay attention to the top four to six inches of growth. There will be anywhere from eight to twelve side branches. These are pinched or pruned back two to three leaf nodes from the main stem. These are forced to break out and as they grow, continue to pinch or prune back the new growth two to three leaf nodes from the last cut. This creates dense thick growth. You will usually have to do this pinch-back / let-it-grow process at least two to three times to create a young standard. Whether creating a standard or a formal topiary, the process is the same up until this point. Then the requirements change.

To continue creating a standard, allow the plant to go through a flowering cycle, after which you will cut it back to just before the last cut. From here, allow it to grow back into a full specimen. As this cycle of pruning, growth, and flowering is repeated, the crown will become fuller and thicker until it reaches maturity. A standard may take anywhere from six months to two years to create. The shorter in height, the faster a standard can be created.

If your standard is a formal topiary such as a myrtle ball, then the pinching process continues as you develop shape and size. Allow the formal topiary to grow out an inch or two, and then prune to one-half the growth. This cutting allows the growth to constantly break out. In time, the pruning becomes a technique of shearing and sculpturing the ball until it reaches maturity (Fig. 4.3). It is best to perform this process of growing out and pruning back regularly, otherwise the branching structure becomes weak and loose. Big holes in the shape may appear with the form falling apart as the plant matures. Varieties that make impressive formal topiaries are Myrtle, Westringia, Rosemary and Serissa. These fine-leafed plants break well and hold their form.

Fig 5.1

Fig 5.3

Once you have created a standard or topiary, then comes the issue of maintenance. Periodically, all standards need to be cut back severely. The everbloomers or seasonal bloomers can be pruned back to near the last cuts. Prune back close to where the initial cuts were made. This will leave the specimen bare with three-quarters or more of the foliage gone. However, whether an everbloomer or a seasonal bloomer, your standard will grow back with more health and vigor, delighting the eye once more.

Formal topiaries or balls also need severe pruning to maintain proportionate size to the height of the plant and pot size. Hence, a top-heavy ball in a small pot would look just as funny as a small ball in a large pot. Hard pruning can be done by cutting back into woody, leafless stems and removing three inches or more of growth. We recommend pruning when plants are growing vigorously.

Stiff-Stemmed Vines

We recommend training vines on a stake, trellis, or hoop. You can also train them around a windowsill with support, a fence post, wire fence or on supports in conservatory structures. Vines need to be pruned when the older growth defoliates or when they become unruly and need to be contained (Fig. 5.1). When pruning, we are always looking at ways to bring it back to a contained fullness.

There are two ways to prune. First, you can severely cut back to any point that removes a large percentage of the foliage and the bulk of the vining stems. This is considered a severe pruning. The look is bare but it does give the plant a fresh start and allows the plant to be re-trained (Fig. 5.2). Second, you can selectively prune. Take one

Fig 5.2

of the growing tips, whether on a stake or trellis, and follow it back to where it initially broke out or sprouted out of an older stem. Remove it (Fig. 5.3). This process is repeated again and again until the plant is thinned and the size reduced.

We often prune seasonal bloomers severely. We typically perform severe pruning once the flowering cycle is complete. This timing allows the plant to re-flower on schedule. However, with everbloomers, we selectively prune some of the stems, allowing flowers to continue on the growing tips. Two everbloomers that benefit from selective pruning are Bougainvillea and Passionflowers. Selective pruning helps thin and manage the specimen.

pruning

Containers

- **The potted plant**

- **Types of pots**
  clay
  wood
  plastic
  glazed ceramic
  cement

The Potted Plant

A wide variety of containers are available, all for love of the potted plant. When choosing a container, keep in mind that you are creating a soil environment for the root system. If you can provide an optimum environment for the roots, you will have a healthy plant. This is the most important concept for successful container plants.

For the home gardener, there is a range of pots, from the traditional in shape and form to those with elaborate designs.

Pot Requirements

For a healthy root system, water must be able to pass quickly through the potting mix. Holes in the bottom of pots for drainage are essential. For short-term use, it is possible to grow in 2¼-inch clay pots without holes, but you must be extremely careful with watering. If the pot size is any bigger without holes, or if the use is to be long-term in a hole-less pot, then you may run into trouble with root rot or high fertilizer salt levels.

Some pots have side drainage holes which work fine, too. Traditional clay pots typically have one hole in the bottom. We believe that the clay pot, in most circumstances, is the best long-term container.

Clay Pots

Clay pots have always had a decided advantage. They have better drainage and there is better movement of air into the soil. Air and water have the ability to move through the bottom and sides, allowing the soil to dry more quickly between waterings.

After a plant is watered and the water drains out, spaces are created between the particles of soil as the soil dries. Air moves into the potting mix where there is an exchange of carbon dioxide from the root system. This movement of air and exchange of carbon dioxide is essential to maintain a healthy root system.

A clay pot has a wicking action through its sides that facilitates this action. The formula goes like this: more air exchange means a drier root environment, which means less opportunity for root diseases.

Only fifteen years ago at Logee's, we were growing everything in clay pots. However, the disadvantage and impracticality was seen in the increased handling cost and breakage. Clay pots are more expensive than plastic. We decided, for commercial use, we would use plastic.

However, plants that we don't ship and that are used for display purposes always get clay pots. In addition to better aeration, the aesthetics of red earthenware clay are more pleasing. They come in all shapes and sizes, from the tall, deep pots used for standard culture or half-pots, to the clay pan pots used for bulbs. Some of the more attractive clay pots have rolled rims, imprint designs and now even come in a variety of shapes.

We have a pair of outstanding tub clay pots that were imported from Italy over 100 years ago. Each spring, we put the Bay Bushes in these four-foot high containers which grace either side of the Lathe house. Every fall, we take the soil out and tip them over so they shed water and make it through the winter without cracking.

Plastic Pots

Plastic is inexpensive, lightweight, and functional. And it comes in wide varieties of shapes, sizes, and colors. With the proper soil mix and attentive watering, plants do well in plastic pots. Ninety-nine percent of the horticultural industry uses plastic, as seen in bedding plants and holiday plants. We use plastic pots for short term growing.

However, for plants that are sensitive to root disease, trouble can arise in a plastic container. Plastic holds moisture longer, leaving plants that are susceptibile to root rots exposed. Particular attention must be given to watering. When any environmental stress occurs, such as high humidity or cool temperatures, beware.

We don't recommend plastic self-watering containers. The reservoir of water that wicks into the soil never allows the plant to dry out and may cause an unhealthy root environment.

If you tend to over-water, use clay. If you tend to under-water, plastic may be fine. Experiment with it. Many people grow in plastic successfully and, with proper watering and an open potting mix, most plant genera will grow well.

Wood

Wood containers are rarely used today. However, there are still those who use large wooden tubs, half barrels, or containers made of redwood, cypress, or cedar. Wooden window boxes or troughs are still popular for displaying summer plants as well.

Wood often drains better than plastic but does not have the wicking advantage of clay. At one time, many wood containers were coated with creosote, which not only eventually killed the plant, but was also a toxic carcinogen for people. Today, pressure-treated wood is used with few harmful side effects. Although decorative, wood decays with time and is heavy to lift, especially when water-logged. However, there is an appeal to planting cascading beauties against a natural wood setting.

Cement Containers

Cement containers are formed like cast lawn ornaments. Cement is not used much today, although there are still the cement urns and troughs seen at cemeteries or the entrances of estates. Cement has the obvious disadvantage of weight, and it is not as porous as clay. But we have seen attractive displays of plants in cement containers. They are just not as practical for the home or patio.

Glazed Containers

Glazed containers have become popular because of their decorative designs. The main disadvantage is that glazing is nonporous, creating a moisture barrier. Glazed pots are similar to plastic in not allowing the root system to breathe.

The advantage to glazed pots is that they are highly decorative and inexpensive. Glazed ceramics work well as *jardinieres*. They are large enough to fit around a clay pot and make an attractive design. The most famous jardinieres in New England are Bennington pottery. The rich, brown glazing with a sometimes three-foot glazed stand is not only attractive but also very valuable in the antique world.

Remember, if you're going to grow in a glazed pot, be sure there is a drainage hole. Jardinieres do not typically have drainage holes; therefore, do not directly pot a plant in them.

containers

Pests and Disease

- *Plant Symptoms*

- *Identification*

- *Management*

  Aphids
  Mites
  Mealy bug
  Scale
  Thrip
  White fly
  Snails and Slugs
  Foliar Disease
  Root Disease

PESTS

Wherever there are plants, there are insects and diseases that feed on them. As gardeners, we will always be faced with insects that feed on our plants and diseases that challenge the plants' growth. All insects can be dealt with efficiently and effectively with a few simple steps. You don't ever need to throw a plant out. Basically, three choices are available when dealing with insects.

First, you can leave the insect on your plant. This is not an option for us because we are in the shipping business and pride ourselves on supplying our customers with a clean plant. But in the home environment, you can simply leave the insects alone. Second, you can use sprays to kill, repel, or subdue the pests on your plants, or third, you can use predatory insects to control the unwanted pests.

Insects come from somewhere. They don't spontaneously generate. The most common way of getting pests on your plants is after they've summered outdoors and are then brought inside for the cooler months. When this change in environmental conditions takes place, the insect population explodes.

Another common way pests are brought to your plants is when you introduce new plants into your collection. At times, these plants are not clean. The gardener, whether hobbyist or commercial, did not intentionally infest the plant with bugs. Many times, if the plant had an invisible, residual population of eggs or crawlers, the plant can begin an infestation of insects. We always suggest isolating a new plant before bringing it into contact with your other plants.

If you don't isolate new plants, then your other varieties in your collection are at risk. Why? Because some pests are extremely mobile, such as spider mite or white fly. Although certain pests do prefer certain plants, it is best to give new plants several weeks of close scrutiny. With a little pest management, your green collection can remain healthy and vibrant.

The first most important step to insect control is identification of the insect. We suggest a 5x or 10x magnifier. Once identified, the next most important step is managing the insect while not harming the plants' ability to grow. We will cover seven groupings of insects that feed on container or greenhouse plants. Under each heading, you will find information on how to identify the pest and how to manage an infestation.

Aphids
PLANT SYMPTOMS

Aphids are found on the soft growing tips or the undersides of the leaves. They feed on the sugars of the plant. When populations are high, they excrete a sticky substance on the leaves, which is called "honey dew." Plants that are more susceptible to aphids are those that have been forced to grow quickly with high amounts of fertilizer. The lush growth produces excess sugars, which in turn provides more sugar for the aphids to feed on. If the sticky substance or sugar sits on the leaves too long, a sooty mold will grow, making the leaves unsightly.

IDENTIFICATION OF APHIDS

Aphids are also known as "plant lice." The most common variety of aphids found on container plants is the "Peach Aphid." The adult is usually colored green, although they can be dark in color. Its method of reproduction is odd in the insect world in that it reproduces in two ways. It grows from an egg into an adult, like most other insects, but adult aphids also give birth to mature insects. Therefore, these two mechanisms of reproduction make the population increase rapidly.

One visible sign of an aphid population is the appearance of a white chafe covering on the leaves of the plant. These are the skins of the molting insects. Upon closer inspection, you will find live adults clustering on the young growth.

MANAGEMENT OF APHIDS

Outbreaks generally happen in late winter and early spring. Management of aphids is challenging because of their asexual reproduction, and because of their ability to mutate through pesticides.

A small or a large population of aphids won't kill a plant, although a large population can make the foliage unsightly. The downside of leaving a few aphids in a home situation is that, at any time, the population can grow. Aphids are generally not a problem outside because other predators and environmental factors take care of them. There are several methods to controlling aphids.

Synthetic Compounds

The synthetic compounds that we are presently using for aphids are called Endeavor and Marathon, but by the time of this reading, the pest, more than likely, will have mutated through these products.

Nicotine

Nicotine is the best defense against aphids. Take a pack of unfiltered cigarettes and soak everything, the paper included, in 1 quart of water overnight. The next day, strain, and add a dribble of dishwashing deter-

Aphids: Visible adults as well as the characteristic white chaff or skins left from molting.

gent to the liquid. The detergent breaks the surface tension so when you spray, the insect gets coated. Put the liquid in a spray bottle and

pests and disease

perform two applications. Spray one week apart and spray the entire plant. Make sure to coat the top and the bottom of the leaves of the plant. The phrase we use in the industry is, "spray until run off." Remember that aphids are mostly on the growing tips. If this method doesn't control aphids, then either the insect was missed by the spray, or the strength of the nicotine in the mixture was not potent enough.

Spider mites: *The clear light peppering or pin pricks are symptomatic of early spider mite infection.*

Predators

Two predators that we've experimented with are a small, harmless wasp called *Aphidius colemani* and the larvae of the lacewing. The larvae feed on the aphids and consume many of them. If the population is not entirely consumed, then the predators continue reproducing, laying eggs and consuming more aphids. In time, the predators win out and the aphids disappear. Then, the larvae don't have any more food to eat, so they too die. This method does work. However, it takes time and a vigilant eye to make sure that other pests don't get out of hand before their work is done. When using predatory insects, broad spectrum insecticides must be avoided.

Mites

PLANT SYMPTOMS

The spider mite is usually found on the underside of the leaves. The first symptoms are tiny little dots or peppering seen on the leaves. They are clear or colored dots that look like tiny pinpricks. It is best to identify spider mite at this stage because management will be much easier. As populations grow, webbing will start to cover the plant. The leaves become pale in color and, if not treated, the plant will defoliate.

The cyclamen mite is found on the growing tips and can turn the growing tips black. Also, a stunting and distortion of the young leaves

is visible as they grow out. Cyclamine mite are prevalent on African violets and other gesneriads and occasionally on begonias.

IDENTIFICATION OF MITES

Two mites cause damage to greenhouse and conservatory plants. One is the two-spotted spider mite, also called the red spider mite. The second type is the broad mite, also called the cyclamine mite. We treat them the same yet, in recent years, we mostly see spider mites. As their name implies, they look like tiny spiders and only feed on certain plant species.

Cyclamine mites are small. Use a 10x magnifier for proper identifi-

plant care

cation. Slow moving, clear or brown-bodied pests will be found on the growing tips of the plant. Sometimes they are missed because of their ability to camouflage with the leaf structure.

MANAGEMENT OF MITES
Neem Oil
The best product we have for the home gardener is the pure *Neem Oil*, by Dyna-Gro. This oil is very effective because it mechanically smothers the adult and the eggs of the mite but, unlike other oils, does no damage to the plant. One application is usually sufficient but we always recommend two, spaced out between five to seven days. The amount that is most effective is 1 ounce (2 tablespoons) of Neem Oil to 1½ teaspoons of dishwashing detergent. Again, the detergent emulsifies the oil allowing it to dissolve in the water.

Of the 1,500 varieties of plants that we grow, we advise caution using Neem Oil with only one: The Golden Flax plant (*Reinwardia indica*) experienced small amounts of damage. Neem Oil is a safe, organic product. It is the oil from the neem seed, a tropical tree, and has many other uses in the cosmetic and lubricant industry.

Predators
The use of predatory mites to control spider mite infestation is highly effective. Two predatory mites, *Pyytosieulus persimilis* and *Neoseiulus californicus*, work well on greenhouse and interior plants. Adult predatory mites are released on the infested plants where they then consume spider mites at a rapid rate. We've used them with great success. It is important to release the predators at the first signs of infestation as it takes several weeks for them to gain control. Again, do not spray with broad-spectrum insecticides at this time.

Mealy Bugs
PLANT SYMPTOMS
Mealy bugs tend to prefer certain plant species. One of the signs of mealy bugs is a cottony mass on the leaf axes or the underside of the leaves. Once you've seen this, you know the plant has mealy bugs.

IDENTIFICATION OF MEALY BUGS
There are several types of mealy bugs, such as citrus mealy bugs and long-tailed mealy bugs. However, we treat all mealy bugs the same. They are one of the most challenging pests to control on container plants. The problem arises from the life cycle of the insect. The stages from egg to adult are extended, meaning not all of the eggs will develop at the same rate. Also, mealy bugs have the ability to hide. Eggs are laid inside the cottony mass, which is often hidden in cracks or crevices behind plant stems. Once the eggs hatch, microscopic orange crawlers move out to the leaves. These are not visible to the naked eye. The juvenile and adults feed on the plant sugars. In heavy infestations, they will excrete the sugars onto the leaf surface, which in time will cause a black, sooty mold to develop. Adults are covered with a waxy, white coating, which is often impervious to water. The cottony mass is also impervious to water. The only time this insect is vulnerable is during its crawling stage; however, because of its extended life cycle, all the crawlers don't come out at once. In addition, populations can expand rapidly without being seen. Often, a plant infested with mealy bug will be sprayed once or twice. For a while, this takes care of the problem, but within three to six months, mealy bugs suddenly reappear.

pests and disease

Mealybugs: The white cotton masses found at the leaf axis and underside of leaf as well as visible adults.

MANAGEMENT OF MEALY BUGS
Alcohol

The long standing treatment has been to dip a Q-tip in alcohol and then dab the cottony mass. However, this method is only somewhat effective because it often misses the crawler.

Instead, make a spray of 50% water and 50% isopropyl alcohol. Then spray the entire plant. The trick is to use enough force to dislodge and penetrate the cottony masses and the waxy coating on the adults. A hand sprayer is not adequate. We recommend a pump sprayer with pressure. This will also get into the crevices of the plant. On some plants, like clivias or the calyx of a flower, any amount of spraying will not get all the spots.

Sprays

Mealy bugs are one of the few insects that we still battle with broad-spectrum synthetic pesticides. A Dursban product, called *Duragard*, which is safe for the handler, is an organophosphate compound. Add Dursband to the alcohol solution spray listed above, and use a pump sprayer with enough pressure to dislodge the cotton mass. Repeat applications once a week for three weeks or, if temperatures are cool, for four weeks in a row. This will allow the vulnerable crawlers to move out of the cotton mass. Again, dislodge the mass with pressure.

Oils

Ultrafine Oil, or Neem Oil, is effective for the crawling stage of the mealy bug, but has little affect on adults.

With alcohol and oils, mealy bugs can be controlled in a home environment without using hard poisons. The most frequent mistake is stopping after one or two applications. With mealy bugs, you must be persistent. Much like taking an antibiotic, it's always recommended to finish the prescription, even after you feel better. The same applies to mealy bugs; long after you've seen the last bug, finish the four-week cycle of pressurized spraying.

Predators

Cryptolaemus, a lady beetle from Australia, specifically feeds on mealy bugs. Its larvae feed on all stages of the mealy bug. For this predator to be successful, a high infestation of mealy bugs must be present.

The lady beetles are expensive, but well worth the money when effective. We've released them in our greenhouses a number of times. Once they worked well, but another time they only worked intermittently. We recommend them for a small conservatory or greenhouse. It takes time to acquire good control. The most time consuming requirement is that plants cannot be sprayed for sixty days with harsh pesticides before the introduction of predators. Unfortunately, in our business world, we are unable to wait sixty days and still keep up with our clean plant requirements.

Scale

PLANT SYMPTOMS

Scale appears on certain types of plants such as citrus, bay, mitriostigma, and ferns. Scale is camouflaged and sits along the stem. The first evidence appears as honey dew on leaves. With close examination, brown bumps can be found on the stems and leaves. They can be scraped off with your fingers.

IDENTIFICATION OF SCALE

"Greenhouse scale" is the most common scale found on container plants. Under the bumps that appear on the stems and the leaves are the eggs and the crawlers. Here they are protected from sprays, and when they do crawl out, they are invisible to the eye. They attach themselves to the leaf and form the soft-shell stage of the insect. They continue to grow, but they are clear in color and difficult to detect. However, this, along with the crawlers, is the most vulnerable stage. If scale are caught during this vulnerable stage, then better control can be gained.

MANAGEMENT OF SCALE

Again, the problem with scale is that they are difficult to detect, and they are protected under the brown bumps. When they do crawl out, much like mealy bug, they crawl out over a long period of time. This means persistent spraying is necessary for control.

Spray

Scale is not as mobile as other pests but it still needs to be sprayed. A spray we recommend for shiny-leafed plants is called *Cedoflora*. It's very effective in controlling scale and it is safe. It does require several applications, however. *Cedoflora* should be used with caution on soft-leafed plants because often times it will damage the leaves. This is called *phytotoxicity*.

Orthene, which we rarely use, is a powerful and poisonous synthetic pesticide. One application can kill all stages. It works systemically and translocates, meaning it is absorbed through the leaf. Wherever the insect is feeding, it will digest the poison. Orthene has an awful odor and must be used with caution.

We were scale free for over ten years, but recently, several of our stock plants had an outbreak, but only on the shiny-leafed variety. Overall, we recommend Cedoflora for its low toxicity, safe use, and

Scale: The brown bumps and the scale like soft shell stage visible on the leaf and stem.

effectiveness. The good news is that scale generally prefer only the shiny-leafed plants.

Oils

Pure Neem Oil is also used effectively but must be reapplied over a period of four to eight weeks. We recommend this for non-shiny leaves, but since it does not get under the bumps, we also recommend spraying twice a month for two months. The amount that is most effective is 1 ounce (2 tablespoons) of Neem Oil and 1½ teaspoons of dishwashing detergent added to 1 gallon of water. Again, the detergent emulsifies the oil.

Thrip

PLANT SYMPTOMS

The best indicator of thrip is if the edges of the flowers start to discolor and become thin and dry. Damage to the overall plant is usually not an issue, unless populations get extremely high. Then, the leaves can start to turn bronze or there are small spots from the lost chlorophyll in the leaf. Thrip leaf damage is larger than spider mite damage. Thrip seem to be attracted to blue flowers, which can also be an indicator of their presence.

Thrip: Patchy light areas of lost chlorophyll from the feeding adults.

IDENTIFICATION OF THRIP

Thrip is hard to see with the naked eye but can be done. Thrip is a mobile insect that is torpedo-shaped and has a long life cycle. It hides in the flowers and other parts of the plants that contact sprays miss. It feeds on flowers and other parts of the plants. Peel apart flowers, and with a magnifier, look inside for the adult.

Like most insects, it has an egg-to-adult life cycle. Eggs are laid in the soil. The larvae pupate in about 30 days. They hatch and feed on plant tissue and flowers. When they are in the egg stage in the soil, they are impossible to see. When they are adults, they can be diffi-cult to find. The best place to find thrip is on the flower when they're feeding.

MANAGEMENT OF THRIP

Thrip has been around for a long time but never became a problem until about fifteen years ago when greenhouses were invaded by the western flower thrip. They are known vectors of virus, which means they transmit virus from plant species to plant species. Thrip needs to be controlled for this factor alone. The best way that we control thrip populations is by fogging or fumigating. Since they are hard to see and because their mobility is so great, we simply smoke the entire greenhouse, targeting thrip as the main pest to eradicate.

Most home environments don't have to use such drastic measures, however. We recommend three products for home use.

Neem Oil

The amount that is most effective is to add 1 ounce (2 tablespoons) of Neem Oil and 1½ teaspoons of dishwashing detergent to 1 gallon of water. You can also drench with Neem Oil. Drenching is a technique where you use the mixture above along with additional water and simply drench, or water, the plant with it. Spraying and drenching both control the egg and pupa stage in the soil and the adult stage. The downside is that you must constantly and consistently reapply the sprays weekly for four weeks.

Conserve

A new product called *Conserve* is a biologically, environmentally sound pesticide. Conserve is effective against thrip and catepillars.

Orthene

We don't use Orthene because of its odor and indiscriminate killing of all insects. It is not environmentally friendly.

Predators

There are predators available for thrip; however, they are not as reliable.

White Fly

PLANT SYMPTOMS

You know you have white fly when you brush up against a plant and white clouds of tiny flies emerge. Another plant symptom is little, scar-like bumps found on the underside of the leaves. When the populations get high, sticky honeydew falls on the leaves and, in time, they are colonized by sooty mold causing blackened leaves. Yet even with substantial populations of white fly, the plants go on living but are not as vigorous or healthy as they could be. Some leaf distortion will occur in high populations. At Logee's, we've never seen a plant die from white fly, but the infestations can be a nuisance. The sticky honeydew not only covers the plant, but drips on anything nearby.

White fly like a wide variety of plants such as Abutilons, Hibiscus, Thunbergias, Mints, Salvias, Brugmansias, Daturas and Cestrums.

IDENTIFICATION OF WHITE FLY

The visible insect is a small white fly that is mobile. It lives on the underside of the leaves. The entire white fly life cycle takes place on the underside of the plant's leaves. The bumps on the leaves are the pupating white fly.

The life cycle on average lasts thirty to thirty-four days from egg to mated adult, depending on the temperature. In egg form or crawler form, they can't be seen with the naked eye. Crawlers attach themselves to the leaf and then go through several enstar stages of growth and pupation. An enstar stage is when the insect cocoons, then sheds and molts its outer skin. Throughout their life cycle, the white flies are feeding on the plant tissue. Once white flies becomes adults, they mate and lay eggs again.

Several varieties affect container plants. We treat them all the same. However, the most aggressive species is the sweet potato white fly.

MANAGEMENT OF WHITE FLY

The difficulty in treating white fly is much like aphids; they have the ability to rapidly mutate through pesticides. They do have vulnerable stages, however — the egg stage and the crawler stage. During the adult stage, they are far too mobile. We recommend sprays directed toward the vulnerable stages, and after about thirty days, there will no longer be adults.

Sprays

We recommend sprays or insecticides that affect the egg, crawler, and enstar stage of growth. The adult stage will somewhat be affected also. When we have worked only with adulticides (pesticides targeted for the adult insect), it is a thirty-day process.

Neem Oil

Neem Oil works well because it smothers the eggs and the crawlers.

Whitefly: The adult whitefly and the scale like immature pupae found on the underside of the leaf.

The same pesticide, also called *Pyro Grow*, is in a microencapsulated formulation. What this means is that the chemical is encapsulated in a tiny bead. When wet, the chemical stays inside the bead, which makes it extremely safe for anyone handling the product. Once Pyro Grow is sprayed on the leaf and then dries, the capsule bursts and releases the pesticide.

This product has been so effective that we, literally, have had no white fly in the greenhouses for the past three years. Soon, though, we expect that the white fly will mutate through this pesticide also. However, it is not necessary to have such clean plants in a home environment, so we still recommend Neem Oil for its reliability and organic nature.

Predators

The most effective predator for controlling white fly is a tiny wasp called *Encarsia formosa*, which feed on the white fly nymph.

It also works as an insect growth regulator on the enstar stage. The amount that is most effective is to add 1 ounce (2 tablespoons) of Neem Oil and 1½ teaspoons of dishwashing detergent to 1 gallon of water. Again, the detergent emulsifies the oil. With several applications of Neem Oil spray, the adult population will recede and disappear altogether.

Synthetic Growth Regulator

We have found a product called *Distance* that is effective. It is safe, has low toxicity, and is specific.

plant care

Snails and Slugs

PLANT SYMPTOMS

The first noticeable sign of snails or slugs show up as holes chewed in the leaves. Whenever holes appear, it's usually indicative of these hungry pests. The undeniable sign is the slippery trail of slime found up and down the stems. Snails and slugs tend to munch on soft plants, such as Ferns, Hibiscus, and Passionflowers, actually preferring individual cultivars to others.

IDENTIFICATION OF SLUGS

Remember turning over logs and finding slimy slugs? They're no different than greenhouse or container plant slugs. Overall, they are less of a pest, mostly because they're visible to the eye and can be mechanically removed.

Greenhouse slugs grow to approximately one-inch in length and are soft-bodied insects. Snails have the same characteristics, but have a shell on their back. Both like to hide during the daytime and stay in the damp, wet areas such as pot drainage holes or the bottom of the pots. They lay eggs in these places, which show up as little clear beads.

MANAGEMENT OF SLUGS AND SNAILS

Remove

Mechanically remove the slugs or snails.

Pellets or Bait

For the faint of heart, simply get slug pellets or snail bait. Dribble the bait on the soil where they can feed on the poison, which eventually kills them.

Slugs in our greenhouses are around but don't seem to bother the plants. They seem to be our friendly pests and climb around the beds, feeding on the algae. Occasionally, we have to put out a few pellets for control, especially on susceptible varieties. If you choose to use pellets, remember to handle the pellets with care.

Copper

Slugs and snails detest copper. They will not cross copper. For a non-toxic approach, use copper flashing or copper wire and put around your pot. Copper acts as a wonderful barrier.

Beer

No, snails and slugs are not social creatures. But it is true that slugs and snails like beer. Put a ½-inch deep saucer filled with beer near your plant. The taste of beer entices the insects to drink themselves silly, until they drown.

pests and disease

FOLIAR DISEASE

At Logee's and throughout indoor container horticulture, we work with basically two foliar diseases. They are mildew and botrytis, which causes blossom blight or leaf spots. Other organisms, such as pseudomonas bacteria, alternaria, and septoria, cause leaf spots and necrosis to the leaf tissue, but they are not as common and are only found in a few species or in extremely damp conditions.

Mildew: The white mold or powder found on the upper leaf surface typical of this foliar disease.

Mildew

PLANT SYMPTOMS

Mildew only effects certain types of plants. The most susceptible types are all begonias, especially rexes, roses, and rosemary. A white fuzz forms on the leaf surface, which is the mildew.

How do plants get mildew?

Mildew is an airborne fungus that germinates and grows under certain environmental conditions. Often a change of season, such as the onset of cooler nights, coupled with higher humidity, will cause mildew. If you grow begonias or roses, you will eventually get to know mildew.

TREATMENT

If not treated early, mildew can consume an entire plant. The spores are generally present and widespread. Environmental conditions encourage infections. The safest method of control is the use of Neem Oil or baking soda.

Neem Oil

Start with one gallon of water and mix in 1 ounce (2 tablespoons) of Neem Oil and 1½ teaspoons of liquid dishwashing detergent. Use in a spray bottle and apply once a week for two weeks. An active infection can be controlled with this formula.

Baking Soda

Start with 1 quart of water and mix in 1 tablespoon of baking soda with a small dribble of dishwashing detergent. The dishwashing detergent breaks surface tension so the mixture will spread easily on the leaves. We recommend using the baking soda mixture as a preventative spray. Apply to susceptible plants quarterly or at the change of seasons. This mixture can also be used for active infections. Spray daily for one week.

Synthetic Spray

Baylaton is a synthetic fungicide used for many foliar diseases and works well on mildew. Commercially, Baylaton is sold as *Strike*.

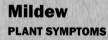

Botrytis

PLANT SYMPTOMS

Botrytis is one of the most prevalent foliar diseases in greenhouse plants. At Logee's, people often comment on how good the high humidity feels, when in reality, it is one of the major factors that make greenhouse plants more susceptible to botrytis. The low humidity of a home environment, typically, does not promote botrytis. Commonly called *gray mold*, botrytis shows up as gray fuzz on the flowers and the foliage. This fungus consumes the plant tissue and can result in flower or leaf damage.

Gray mold is the sporing bodies of the fungus erupting out of the dying tissue. Through this mechanism, the fungus regenerates and spreads the mold. The soft growing plants such as begonias and geraniums are highly susceptible to botrytis.

Leaf spots are also a symptom of botrytis. Patches of brown tissue form on the leaves or stems. A necrosis (dying of plant tissue) is seen. The stems will show concentric bands of progressively darker colors as the mycelium of the fungus consumes the leaf tissue. Note: Disease is not always the precursor to dying tissue. Necrotic leaves can result from excess or deficient nutrients, phytotoxicity or mechanical damage. Pesticides or mechanical damage causes phytotoxicity. However, once the damage is done, then the fungus gets a foothold in the tissue and starts to grow. Other factors such as high humidity, stagnant air, and unsanitary conditions also lend to disease.

How do plants get botrytis?

Botrytis develops when environmental conditions change and there is an extended period of high humidity, with cooler temperatures between 48°F - 60°F. Also, if air is stagnant, then there is a greater chance of infection.

TREATMENT

Presently, the only organic control is to clean the plant mechanically, increase airflow, and change the environmental conditions. We suggest watering in the early morning so that the plants have a chance to dry out before the cooler nighttime temperatures. Do not water when wet weather is coming, especially in spring and fall when temperatures are low. Why? Because stormy weather means high humidity. By adjusting the temperature, watering schedule, and pay-

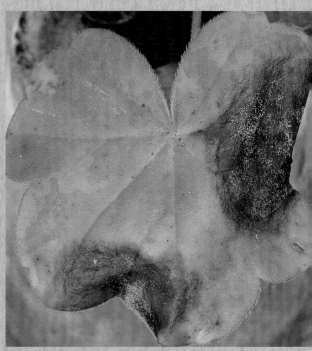

Botrytis: The brown patch of dead tissue and the gray fuzz typical of this foliar disease. Notice it spreads in a circular pattern.

ing attention to sanitation, botrytis should not be a problem.

Botrytis is usually not a problem in a home environment, but can be somewhat tricky in a greenhouse or conservatory. You can also spray with commercial fungicides such as *Decree*.

Environmental Treatment:

Increasing air movement, increasing sanitation, and picking off diseased leaves are some tips that will greatly reduce botrytis leaf spots.

Root disease: The brown roots typical of many of the root pathogens found in container plants. Note the contrasting white roots that are regenerating.

ROOT DISEASE

Roots don't die of old age. They die from disease, improper nutrition, severe drought, and improper watering or excessive amounts of each. We can't over emphasize — *always* examine the root system for health. Some plants are more susceptible to root diseases, such as gardenias and citrus.

PLANT SYMPTOMS

Look for loss of luster in the leaves and a visually stunted plant with less growth on top. There will be a steady decline of the plant. Check the root system for signs. Pull out of pot and examine the roots. Healthy roots should be tan colored with white tips and be succulent and fleshy. Unhealthy roots are brown and brittle. Many times, they will fall apart just from the touch. Also, some of the root diseases will enter the stems, cutting off the flow of water. Sudden leaf drop or severe wilt will result.

How do plants get root rot?

Every container plant has its own environmental conditions within the soil. There are many organisms present in all soil. Just like within our human body, soils and root systems also have levels of bacteria and fungi that are both beneficial and pathological. When imbalances occur, the pathogens get out of hand and disease takes over. There are several prevalent organisms, such as pythium, phytophthora, and rhizoctomia; these are called "water molds" that proliferate under damp conditions.

Like most diseases, the environmental conditions will increase or decrease the susceptibility to root rot. The conditions in the soil, such as the amount of water present, the air exchange, and the length of time moisture is held in the soil are all factors in root disease. Water molds are more active under wet conditions; therefore, it is important to let the plant dry down between watering.

TREATMENT:
Commercial Fungicides

Drench the soil with fungicides. This will suppress the disease for only a short time. There are no curative fungicides.

The best way to control root rot is through culture.

1. Grow in clay pots. Clay helps the soil breathe and moisture is released quickly instead of being trapped.

2. Do not over water. Let the plant dry out some between waterings.

3. Do not over pot the plant. You want the root system to be able to pull moisture out of the soil quickly.

4. Do not use excessive amounts of fertilizer to make plants grow quickly. Too much fertilizer creates soft tissue. The plant cells enlarge, causing a weakened state.

Soils and Fertilizers

- *Soil composition*

- *Fertilizers corrections organic fertilizers*

Soil Ingredients

Potting mixes can keep container plants healthy or they can actually be the cause of a plant's decline. There are many good potting mixes on the market today. We recommend the use of *soil-less* mixes, also called *peat-lite* mixes.

The major components of soil-less mixes are spaghnum peat moss, pearl-lite and vermiculite. Other materials such as southern pine bark are also popular. The combination in soil-less mixes make them open, porous, and well-drained. And, surprisingly enough, these mixes have fairly good nutrients and moisture retention.

We are often asked, "Can I use soil from my garden?" We always answer with an emphatic, NO! Why? The risk for disease is too great. Garden soil is unpasteurized, out of balance, and much too

dense for container culture. Pre-made mixes contain a balance of plant nutrients as well as pH adjustment.

Presently, most of the potting mixes we use at Logee's contain composted pine bark. Beneficial microorganisms are contained in this mix, which help reduce soil-borne diseases.

Soil pH

Another factor in plant health is the soil pH. We grow 99.9% of our plants at a pH of 5.8 - 6.2. Most soil-less mixes have a pH that is slightly acidic. Occasionally, our acid-loving plants, such as the gardenias and camellias, react with symptoms of chlorosis. When this happens, we simply add micronutrients to the potting mix to correct the imbalance.

Some experts recommend the addition of 5 - 10% loam, or topsoil, to the soil-less mixes. Topsoil helps balance or buffer the nutrients in the mix. For short growing times of 12 - 16 weeks, we don't recommend topsoil because imbalances generally are not seen. However, for long term growing,

THREE WAYS TO LOWER THE SOIL PH FOR ACID-LOVING PLANTS

1. Use acid fertilizer that contains ammonium sulfate.

2. Top dress with cotton seed meal.

3. Water with a dilute solution of black tea.

loam helps buffer excessive nutrient imbalances. The down side of using loam in the soil-less mixes is that it creates a heavier mix, hence, air and porosity is reduced. Also, if using loam, it needs to be pasteurized so it is free of weed seeds and pathogens.

Fertilizers

Nutrients are needed to bring any container plant into its fullness. Container growing in soil-less mixes is much like hydroponic growing. In a pot, the plant has a soil environment unto itself and

pests and disease

185

the only way to get the necessary nutrients is from the gardener. When plants are put directly into the ground, they have an ability to expand their root system into new soil, hence expanding their nutrient base.

What is fertilizer?

Fertilizer is material, synthetic or organic, that supplies nutrients to a plant. These nutrients are needed for proper growth of plant tissue, roots, and flowers.

TWO GROUPS

Major nutrients compose the bulk of the fertilizer. NPK — Nitrogen, Phosphate and Potassium — are major plant nutrients. Calcium, magnesium, and sulfur are also considered major plant nutrients, although they are not readily available in commercial fertilizers.

Minor nutrients are necessary for balanced plant health but are only used in small amounts. Presently, the minor nutrients that are thought to be essential are manganese, iron, zinc, molybdenum, and copper.

BALANCED FERTILIZER

A balanced fertilizer simply means that the major nutrients of NPK are close to equal in the mix. For example, a 10-10-10 fertilizer contains 10 parts nitrogen, 10 parts phosphate, and 10 parts potassium. The numbers don't have to be exactly equal. Even a 7-9-5 is considered to be a balanced fertilizer. A good, balanced fertilizer will have the addition of minor nutrients as well. With balanced nutrients, over the long run, nutrient problems are eliminated and proper nutrient levels maintained.

What type of fertilizer is best?

Fertilization of plants is as important as watering them to achieve full, vigorous growth. Remember that a good, balanced fertilizer should have all the major and minor nutrients, also called *macro* and *micronutrients*. Many of the big name fertilizers do not contain all the major or minor nutrients and only contain NPK. We have found an excellent balanced fertilizer called *GROW* by Dynagro. All the major nutrients, including calcium, magnesium, and sulfur, plus the minor nutrients, are included. For the home gardener, Dynagro also produces other products, such as a blossom boosting fertilizer and a foliage fertilizer.

IRON DEFICIENCY OR IRON CHLOROSIS

One of the most common micronutrient deficiencies is seen with iron. Also called *iron chlorosis*, the symptoms appear as an interveinal lightening of the leaf tissue. It is most noticeable on the young leaves. Usually, there is enough iron in the soil, but the plant won't absorb it. Why? Often times, because of other nutrient imbalances, which block the absorption. Another contributing factor is the pH irregularities. Typically, you see chlorosis in acid-loving plants that are growing in too alkaline a soil.

If plants are grown under cold temperatures, below 60°F, for extended periods, nutrient absorption is diminished; hence, iron deficiencies may show up. Also, plants that have diseased root systems lack the ability to absorb iron and iron chlorosis will show up.

There are two ways to correct iron chlorosis. First, try moving the plant into warmer conditions. Second, add *chelated iron* to correct the problem. This form of iron is more readily absorbable, soluble, and mobile. Simply follow the recommendations on the package and dilute in water. Give the plants a drink and splash or mist the leaves.

Iron chlorosis

The foliage and the roots absorb the iron chelate. In one week, if the symptoms have not disappeared, then repeat at weekly intervals until the problem is remedied. When treating with iron chelate, make sure the root system is healthy. The root system must be strong enough to pick up the nutrients.

FERTILIZER RECOMMENDATIONS

Since childhood many of us have heard, "Eat smaller meals more often." The same advice can be applied to feeding your plants. Apply small amounts of balanced fertilizer more often. By using this technique, a couple of things hap-

pen. First, you keep the salt levels, or the build up of excess fertilizer, in check. Second, you overcome the biggest challenge, which is the leaching of plant nutrients out of the soil. With constant, steady supplies of fertilizer, you will be able to produce healthy, vigorous plants.

FERTILIZER CAUTIONS

1. Do not use high amounts of fertilizer to force the growth of your plants. When a plant is forced to grow quicker than it normally would, then the plant tissue becomes soft and more susceptible to insects and disease.

2. With excessive amounts of fertilizer, salt levels rise rapidly and can damage or burn the leaves and the roots. Remember — more is not necessarily better. The symptoms of excessive fertilizers appear as necrotic (dead) tissue that forms in the interveinal areas of the leaves found in the upper parts of the plant, or on the leaf margins. The salt runs up and collects in the tissue. Since the salt gets trapped, the leaf tissue browns and dies. If you see this symptom, stop fertilization immediately. Leach the fertilizers out of the soil simply by running water through the pot.

Organic Fertilizers

The use of organic fertilizers in container horticulture has much merit. Organic fertilizers contain primary nutrients plus a myriad of trace minerals. The main problem with these in container culture is the level of residual nitrogen. Examples of organic fertilizers are fish emulsion, blood meal, and slaughter-house tankage. If used over a long period, a build-up of nitrogen sometimes occurs, which creates leaves rather than flowers.

We highly recommend organic fertilizers. Such natural methods of create sustainability in our

soils and fertilizers

environment. However, to control the imbalances in nitrogen, one option is to intermix salt fertilizers with the organics.

Organic fertilizers come in either liquid or powdered form. Fish emulsion is an excellent liquid fertilizer; however, it usually is overly high in nitrogen. Liquid seaweeds are another option and have a myriad of beneficial trace elements. However, excessive amounts in pot culture can be counter-productive. Use in moderation. The granular or powdered forms are generally not water-soluble and are used as a top dressing.

How to apply fertilizers

Fertilizers can be dissolved in water and applied with each watering. If not soluble, fertilizers can be applied as top dressing, or there are slow-release fertilizers that come in the form of plant sticks or beads. Generally, we don't recommend plant sticks because the fertilizer is concentrated in a small area of the root ball. It is not dispersed throughout the media and the plant does not pull up the nutrients evenly.

Fertilizer beads are used successfully throughout the industry. *Osmocote* and *Nutricote* are trade names of fertilizer beads that work well. The fertilizer is enclosed in a pearl shaped membrane that allows small amounts to leach out into the pot over a period of ninety days or longer. This is an effective way to fertilize.

GUIDELINES FOR FERTILIZER APPLICATION

Low amounts or light feeders:
Lower-light plants or slow-growing plants only need ¼ teaspoon of balanced fertilizers dissolved in 1 gallon of water on weekly or bi-weekly basis, added to the soil when the plants are given a drink. We do not recommend top dressing with soluble salt fertilizers for light feeders because they are too strong.

Moderate amounts or moderate feeders: For fast growers or high-light plants, there are two ways to fertilizer. 1) Give less feed more often, such as ½ – ¾ teaspoon per 1 gallon of water on a weekly basis. 2) Use the continuous feed

method, which is ¼ teaspoon per 1 gallon at every watering. Plants grow rapidly under this type of fertilization. A note of caution with the continuous feeding method: remember to periodically stop the fertilization for a few waterings and give only clear water so salt levels do not build up. Run clear water every couple of weeks.

Top dress is another option for the moderate feeders. Use a slow-release fertilizer and follow the recommendations per pot size.

Heavy amounts or heavy feeders:
For heavy feeders, fertilization is similar to that of the moderate feeders' guidelines except increased somewhat, especially for species such as brugmansias or abutilons. Apply 1 teaspoon per 1 gallon per week. You may also continuous feed, which should be ½ teaspoon per gallon at every watering. Remember to flush with clear water every couple of weeks so the salt levels do not build up.

Watering

One of the most important cultural requirements for container growing is proper watering. Ninety-eight percent of the plants we grow can be watered the same way. First, visually observe the soils' color. If the soil turns from dark to light, then give the plant a drink. The idea is to allow the soil to dry down some between waterings. Drying out the plant allows oxygen to move into the soil spaces. In turn, this creates a healthier root environment. When a plant needs watering, thoroughly saturate the root ball with water to the point where a little water runs out of the drainage holes.

The other way to tell when a plant needs to be watered is by symptoms of wilt or drooping. However, wilt is not always a true indicator of simple water needs because a plant with damaged roots often shows this symptom, especially under high light. A plant with a damaged root system will not take up water. There are also plants, such as fuchsias, that sometimes fool us. Fuchsias may go into a wilt, but it is not because they don't have enough water or because their roots are damaged. It is because they transpire water through their leaves so quickly in hot weather that they go into a wilt.

Severe wilt can be detrimental in most cases and should be avoided. A slight wilt can be beneficial because it tends to strengthen a plant by creating tougher tissue, and because it thoroughly aerates the soil.

Another way to determine if a plant needs to be watered is to feel the soil with your hand. This technique is especially useful for the hanging baskets or for those containers covered by foliage.

Much like caring for a pet or a child, it is important to check plants on a regular basis to see if they need to be watered. As one gardener said, "It's the person who waters that makes the plants grow into healthy specimens."

There are some exceptions where plants need to be kept evenly moist and those are the ones that suffer when the soil becomes dry (ie: the *Marantacaea*, *Osmanthus*, and *Selagimella* families). For plants with these types of specific watering needs, we've given additional information in their individual listings.

soils and fertilizers

Appendix

Trouble-shooting Questions

Why doesn't my plant flower?

The inability to bloom can be caused by several factors. First, light level is the most common factor. If you have a full sun plant that isn't flowering, then move it into full sun.

Second, what type of fertilizer is it getting? If given too much nitrogen fertilizer, then mostly foliage, not flowers, will grow. One family that does not need a lot of fertilizer is Passiflora. You will get vigorous green leaves but not many flowers if over fertilized.

Third, check the blooming cycle. Seasonal bloomers respond to day length change. They need cool nights to initiate buds. Generally, if a plant is a fall, winter or spring bloomer, rest assured that it is responding to either light level or temperature.

Why are the leaves on my plant turning yellow and falling off?

Some plants have seasonal shedding of foliage. If leaf drop is excessive, it may have been caused by severe drought stress. Leaf drop may also occur from being under-fertilized. We find the plants that are well fed are able to hold their leaves better when put under severe drought stress. Hungry plants are more susceptible to leaf drop.

Why do my flowers fall off before they open?

The condition of flowers falling off before they open is referred to as *bud blast*. This has a tendency to occur in Camellias and Passionflowers. Several factors that make these plants more susceptible are the following: inadequate light levels; excessive amounts of fertilizer; nighttime temperatures that are too warm. Phalaenopsis orchids are susceptible to bud blast if their potting media gets too dry.

Why has my plant lost its luster and shine, and some of the leaves are rolling and falling off?

When growing citrus and Gardenias in containers this is a common problem. Other genera are also susceptible. Usually rolled or falling leaves are symptoms of a collapsed root system because of root diseases. There are many different organisms that cause the problem but essentially the results are the same. See chapter on diseases. Sometimes you can save the plant if you immediately regulate the moisture and give it a dry down. We also recommend transferring into a clay container.

How can you tell when the soil is dry?

Soil changes color from darkness (wet) to lightness (dry). At Logee's, we water our plants visually — we simply wait for the soil to change color. The plants are checked daily to see if they are visually dry. There is a point between visually dry and wilt. It is that in-between point when you want to give them a drink. Culturally, slight wilt is helpful at times.

How do I clean dust off the leaves?

In a home situation, spray the leaves with a spritzer or take the plant outside and hose it off. If small enough, take the plant to the sink and spray water on the leaves.

appendix

Why are the green leaves dropping off my plant and what can I do about it?

When green leaves drop off a healthy plant it can be a bit disconcerting. However, rest assured that this can be a common occurrence, especially when plants are brought into a new environment. First, plants brought inside experience a drastic difference in light level and humidity. Once the plant adjusts to the new environment, the problem stops.

Second, extreme drought stress will cause similar symptoms in certain species. Often times, the green leaves are quite dry when they fall. Many times the plant will survive, but the leaves shed because of the severe shock of drought.

Third, root and stem disease also can cause this symptom. The disease actually gets into the vascular system of the stems, resulting in the shedding of green leaves. Always check the root system for healthy roots. If the growing roots and root tips are brown, the roots are dead(see chapter on root disease). Many times the plant will not recover.

Fourth, plants grown under cold temperatures will drop or shed their leaves. Move into warmer temperatures to remedy the problem

Why is the new growth of the leaves coming out crinkled or bumpy?

Usually this happens under the low humidity of winter and is evident as the new leaves unfurl. Increase humidity or live with the crinkled look. Cyclamine mites or broad mites can also cause distorted crinkled growth on certain species. However, there is often some evidence of scarring on the leaf surface(see chapter on pests to manage mites).

What if my plant wilts with the leaves going limp, but the soil is still moist?

More than likely, the root system has collapsed from root disease or excessive watering. The roots are no longer able to take up water. There are some instances in certain plants, under high temperatures, where the transpiration of water is so great that the root system can't keep up. This is a common problem in Fuchsias. If this is the case, adjust watering and move plants to cooler or shadier spots (see chapter on root disease).

What is causing the edges of my leaves to turn brown?

Often called *edge burn*, it can be a complex problem. There are several factors involved. Some of the causes are excessive or deficient nutrients such as calcium, over fertilization or high salt levels, low humidity, poor growing conditions such as low light levels, diseases, or a combination of the above. For plants that are regularly fertilized, eliminate fertilization. Then leach the soil mix. Calcium deficiencies can be corrected by adding *calcium sulfate*, also known as *agricultural gypsum*. Apply as a top dress. If low humidity, increase humidity. Make sure light levels are adequate for growing. Diseases can be corrected by spraying fungicides or changing the environmental conditions.

What is the sticky substance residue on the leaves? What can I do about it?

Usually this is a sign of insect infestation. The sticky substance is called *honeydew* and it is the excretion of sugars from plant sucking insects. First, identify the insect — look to see if they are aphids, mealy bug, white fly or scale. Go to the Pests/Disease chapter in this

trouble-shooting

book and follow the recommendations for managing pests.

My leaves are turning yellow and there is webbing on top of the plant?

Spider mite infestation is at hand. Follow the recommendations in this book on how to control for spider mite.

Why are there patches of brown or dead leaf tissue on some of the leaves of my plant?

There are several causes: over fertilization or excessive salt levels, or it may be the signs of foliar disease. Leaf spots are also caused by *phytotoxicity*, which is a result of pesticide use or some kind of mechanical damage.

Why do the leaves of my plant curl downward?

Leaves that curl downward are typically signs of poor growing conditions. Check the light level; generally it needs to be increased. However, shade-loving plants may need a decrease in light level. Nutrient deficiencies may also be a cause. Make sure plants are given a balanced fertilizer.

Why does my plant only have leaves at the top of the stem and looks like a palm tree?

This is a common problem for plants grown in containers. Excessive drought stress or insufficient soil fertility can cause the shedding of the lower leaves. Fast-growing plants grown in container periodically need to be pruned to restructure growth. Be attentive to watering and make sure the plant is receiving regular applications of a balanced fertilizer.

Sources

The information in this book can be applied to container plants purchased from other nurseries that sell tripical plants. To view our plant collection, you may order a catalog by calling 1-888-330-8038 or 1-860-774-8038, visit our website www.logees.com, or you can write to us at 141 North St., Danielson, CT 06239.

Glossary of Terms

Acidic soil: a pH level less than 7.0 when the soil is tested

Active growth: when a plant is producing leaves, stems and roots

Alkaline soil: a pH level greater than 7.0 when the soil is tested

Axillary bud: a bud found along the stem just above a leaf node.

Blossom blight: the flowers that have blemishes caused by Botrytis

Botrytis: A gray mold or gray fuzz that shows up on leaves or flowers

Bract: technically a leaf although it can be brilliantly colored, ie: Bougainvillea

Bud: there are two types of buds: flower buds grow into flowers; growth buds grow into leaves

Bud Blast: immature flower buds drop off the plant

Chlorosis: an interveinal lightening of the leaf structure, most prevalent in young leaves

Complete Fertilizer: a balance fertilizer that has the three essential nutrients: nitrogen, phosporous, potassium (NPK)

Cultivar: A specific variety that is selected out of cultivation

Cutting: a part of the plant that is cut off, usually a stem, and rooted to make a new plant

Deadheaded: flowers that have wilted and do not fall off that need to be picked off

Deciduous: a plant that drops its leaves seasonally as a normal part of development

Defoliate: when a plant drops all its leaves, often associated with seasonal dormancies

Diseases: Viral, fungal or bacterial organisms that invade the plant and hinder normal development. Symptoms appear as mildews, rots, wilts on the stems, leaves and flowers.

Divide: certain plants that grow by rhizome can be divided to make new plants

Dormancy: a resting period when growth does not occur

Dry down: when a plant is brought to a slight wilt between waterings

Dwarf: a plant that is smaller than the other varieties in the same family

Family: a botanical division known as *genera* (*genus*) within the plant kingdom

Fertilizer: plant nutrients in the form of synthetic or organic compounds

Floriferous: free flowering, producing abundant flowers

Foliage plants: plants that only grow leafs and no flowers

Genus: a botanical division of plants within a family, also called *genera*

Gray mold: used interchangeably with Botrytis, a gray fuzz that covers the leaves of certain plants

Habit: describes growing characteristics such as vining, shrub, or upright

Hardiness zone: The USDA produced a plant hardiness map of North America. The eleven hardiness zones make it easy to tell which plant is tolerant to which zone for outdoor growth.

Hardy: Refers to temperature and the tolerance to or the resistance of outdoor temperatures. Hardy plants are more tolerant to cold temperatures.

Herbaceous: a description for non-woody stemmed plants

Hybrid: cross-pollinating two plants to make a new or superior plant than the combination of the parent plants.

Inflorescence: another term for flower which includes all flower structures such as umbels, spikes and racemes

Internode: the area of the stem between leaf nodes

Iron chelate: an absorbable type of iron used to remedy the problem of iron chlorosis

Iron deficiency: when iron is not absorbed by the roots, the leaves get iron chlorosis

Lead: a terminal shoot off a branch or vining stem

Leaf node: the point along a stem where a leaf joins

Leaf spot: patches of dead tissue usually oval in shape that result from fungus or bacterial pathogens

Leggy: plants that have long, spindly-looking stalks because of low light levels, competition from other plants or over fertilization

Loam: the upper surface of a natural soil usually containing organic matter and humus.

Mildew: a white fuzz that forms on the leaf structure caused by a fungus (roses and begonias are highly susceptible)

Multi-stemmed: many stems arising from a potted plant often created by pruning

Neutral soil: soil that has a pH level of 7.0, neither acidic nor alkaline

Nitrogen: one of the major plant nutrients

Organic matter: decayed living material in a soil

Perennial: plant that comes back or grow year after year

Pests: insects or diseases that attack and feed on the plant

pH: A scale that ranges from 0 to 14 to determine the acidic or alkaline quality of the soil. The lowest end is most acidic, while 14 is most alkaline, and 7.0 is neutral.

Phosphorous: one of the major plant nutrients

Phytotoxicity: when a plant gets damaged by pesticides or mechanical damage

Pinching: a process of pruning young plants with forefingers or scissors to create full bushy specimens

Potassium: one of the major nutrients

Potbound: referring to a container plant whose root ball is thickly matted

Propogate: to reproduce a plant by seed, cutting, graft or division

Pruning: a cutting off growth technique used to create full bushy plants or maintain the shape and size of plants

Raceme: flowers that cluster along a main axis

Repot: taking the plant out of one container and putting it another, usually larger container

Rhizome: the stem of a plant that forms horizontally, usually at the soil surface, from which new roots and leaf stems of the plant form

Root ball: all of the roots held in the container

Root disease: viral, fungal or bacterial organisms that infect the root system, typically refered to as *root rot*

Scraggly: a loose term for the structure and form of a plant that has lost leaves and become thin and unsightly

Seedling: a young plant grown from seed (not a cutting)

Shrub: describing the growth habit of a plant that has nultiple stems arising from the base

Species: A unit of plant classification within a genus. A genus generally has more than one species within it.

Stake: a structure used to support plants so they don't flop over

appendix

Standard: training a specific plant that has a central stem into a form; standards can be either tree-like or formal balls

Succulent: water storing stems or leaves

Suckers: secondary shoots that come off of growth buds on the roots or the stems

Tender: opposite of hardy; the plant is sensitive to or has a low tolerance for cold temperatures

Terminal growth: the highest growing part of a plant comprising stems, leaves and buds

Top dress: refers to applying fertilizer to the surface of the soil, which allows irrigation water to leach in the root system

Topiary: the formal shaping of a plant into a form ie: geometrical designs, animals, etc.

Transpire: a condition where plant leaves let off water

Trellis: a structure that adds support and gives a place for vining plants to grow

Tuber: some plants have tubers which are swollen parts of the stem, usually underground

Umbel: a flower cluster that forms into the shape of an umbrella

Variegated foliage: leaves that have more than one color, usually white or yellow, in some identifiable pattern

Variety: a variant of a species occuring naturally

Vermiculite: a mica-type rock that is used in growing media

Vining habit: descriptive for characteristics of growth habit

Wilt: Usually when water is restricted, plants go into a wilt. Some wilt is helpful; severe wilt can cause plant damage.

Index

index